PENGUIN BOOKS

THE RUNAWAYS

Myron Brenton, a resident of New York City, is the author of several books on medical and health-related matters, including *The American Male, Sex and Your Heart,* and *Friendship.* Other books by him are *The Privacy Invaders, What's Happened to Teacher?,* and *Sex Talk.*

The Runaways is published in association with the editors of *Modern Medicine,* a leading medical journal, and has the endorsement of prominent physicians.

The Runaways

Children, Husbands, Wives, and Parents

by Myron Brenton

PENGUIN BOOKS

Penguin Books Ltd, Harmondsworth,
Middlesex, England
Penguin Books, 625 Madison Avenue,
New York, New York 10022, U.S.A.
Penguin Books Australia Ltd, Ringwood,
Victoria, Australia
Penguin Books Canada Limited, 2801 John Street,
Markham, Ontario, Canada L3R 1B4
Penguin Books (N.Z.) Ltd, 182–190 Wairau Road,
Auckland 10, New Zealand

First published in the United States of America
as A Modern Medicine Book by
Little, Brown & Company 1978
First published in Canada by
Little, Brown & Company (Canada) Limited 1978
Published in Penguin Books by
arrangement with Little, Brown & Company 1979

Library of Congress Cataloging in Publication Data
Brenton, Myron.
    The runaways.
    Reprint of the 1978 ed. published by Little,
Brown, Boston in series: A modern medicine book.
    Includes bibliographical references.
    1. Problem family—United States.
2. Desertion and non-support—United States.
3. Runaway youth—United States. 4. Runaway
wives—United States. I. Title.
HQ535.B74   1979   301.42'7   79-4375
ISBN 0 14 00.5167 8

Printed in the United States of America by
Offset Paperback Mfrs., Inc., Dallas, Pennsylvania
Set in Baskerville

To Diana
as a way of saying —
I love you

Acknowledgments

It's always an author's pleasure to thank, publicly, the people whose expertise, advice and encouragement helped bring his book to fruition. In this case so many people helped — runaways, the family members left behind, mental health professionals in various parts of the country — that it becomes impossible to thank them all by name. Too, for obvious reasons a number of individuals agreed to be interviewed only on the promise of anonymity.

Still, I would like to mention Earl J. Beatt, Family and Children's Service of Minneapolis; Harry Zelinka, Family Service of Los Angeles; Catherine C. Hiatt, Travelers Aid Society of Washington; Charles W. Liddell, Travelers Aid Society of Boston; and Marjory Montelius, Travelers Aid Society of San Francisco. Agency heads all, they were especially thoughtful in arranging for me to interview many of their staff members.

I would also like to give special thanks to my editors, Brian Richard Boylan and Llewellyn Howland III, for their enthusiasm and support, and to psychiatric social worker Anna Waller-Zemon for her careful reading of the manuscript and for her sound suggestions.

To everyone who shared their knowledge or experiences with me, whether anonymously or not, I want to say how grateful I am.

M. B.

Contents

CONTENTS

Part Three: The Adults

6. Vanishing Husbands: Unnerved, Unmanned,
   Undone   97
7. Runaway Wives: Fear, Frustration and
   Fantasy   120
8. Runaways and Left-Behinds: Themes in
   Common   138
9. Other Wanderers: Floaters and
   Oldsters   146

Part Four: Coping

PART ONE:

Our Runaways

I

See Them Go:
A Nation on the Run

Runaways All

In a sense each of us is a runaway. Feeling too pressured or burdened, too bored or frustrated or trapped by life's conditions, we do — we must — at least temporarily make our escapes or fall apart. Getting a high on, taking a vacation, playing hooky from school or job, retreating into reveries, going on a shopping spree, withdrawing from others, engaging in frenetic activity of whatever kind, even getting sick — all can, under certain circumstances, be construed as a kind of running away.

Some people, acutely aware of their emotional needs, deliberately structure their lives so that there is room for "running away." A middle-aged wife in the Dedham, Massachusetts, area exemplifies this type. The lady lives in a large, rambling house with her husband and children — but maintains a small apartment in a nearby town.

"It's my sanctuary, a place I can run to when things pile up too much for me at home," she explained.

Here is the point: when our connection to our world becomes too taut, too tense, when it brings an overload of stress and anxiety, we simply have to get away. In fact, physiologically we're so programmed that in reaction to stress we mobilize internally, get ready to "fight or flee" — and we're not always ready (or able) to fight.

From another perspective still, most if not all of us are runaways. We fantasize about running away. One of the humanistic mottoes emanating from the Nixon White House was, "When the going gets tough, the tough get going." Yes, a macho wise-guy expression as the Nixon team meant it. But another interpretation is possible. When the going gets tough, too tough, even the toughest among us have to get going — away from there, even if only for the moment, to an easier, safer or more fulfilling place.

And so, if we can't leave physically, we depart on those wings of fancy. The tense, harried vice president in charge of sales has his dreams of chucking it all to live out the rest of his days on Tahiti. The bored, emotionally undernourished housewife dreams of running off with Robert Redford. Not a few people are explicit in their runaway fancies when they have them — to the point of working out in their heads where they would go, how they would dress. According to his widow, even Franklin Delano Roosevelt had his runaway fantasies: in her autobiography, *This I Remember,* Eleanor Roosevelt describes one of FDR's favorite little amusements — trying to figure out how one could vanish with $50,000.

Also among us, in larger numbers than might be reckoned, are the women and men, the girls and boys, who actually do take off, split, run, bolt, desert — the ones who do pack up and flee, leaving spouses, children or parents behind. There is a genuine runaway subculture out there, huge and varied.

How huge can't be defined with any real precision. Who counts runaways? No agency — not on a local police, state or federal level — does so accurately. The FBI's Uniform Crime Reports has a juvenile runaway category, but this merely reflects police figures, and many police departments don't bother to report. As of early 1976 the National Crime Information Center was just beginning to develop a computerized index of missing persons — and then only on the physically and mentally disabled, on involuntary disappearances where danger exists, and on minors. The husband who says, "I'm just going down to the corner to mail a letter, dear," and keeps on walking, will definitely not be represented.

By their very nature, runaways do not lend themselves to an accurate count. Many go underground. Many don't seek help from either the established social service or the alternative helping agencies. None volunteers for the census count with the proclamation, "I am a runaway." There are guesses, projections, though only for juvenile runaways. Still, it is probably no exaggeration to state that, young and old and in-between, there are several million of them out there, the runners, skippers, bolters and floaters of all types.

Who Are the Runaways?

Steve is a runaway. He is forty-five and Austrian-born. It was in 1971 that he, his wife and his two children immigrated to the United States. He didn't arrive poor. He rented an expensive house in Westchester County, close to New York City, set himself up in an import-export business, and lived the good life — until the economic downturn soured things for him as for so many other people. His financial problems snowballed; he went heavily into debt. He and his wife, never shining examples of matrimonial togetherness, started to brawl noisily. His kids, taught to respect him for the money he made, now showed him obvious disrespect. One day he told his best friend, his sole intimate, "I feel like I'm being buried alive." On another occasion he said, "I can't take much more." He hinted gloomily at suicide. Then came a long-expected eviction notice; they were throwing him out of his house for nonpayment of rent. He didn't show the notice to his wife. But two days later he cleaned out his bank account, which had just $250 of borrowed money in it, and vanished. He hasn't been heard from since.

Martha is a runaway. People generally knew her as the wife of a successful San Francisco accountant. She knew herself as an artist who taught art in private schools and had had one show of her own. For years and years Martha fought an inner war over those two views of herself — Martha as the dutiful wife and mother of a very demanding family, Martha as the dedicated artist. She was contemptuous of her husband's work, and he of hers; sometimes he said, "If it weren't for the money I make you'd be just another starving artist." One day she disappeared. She took a few things — clothes, her artist's materials — but left no note to mark her running away. Her family didn't hear from her for nearly a year; then, through a friend, she finally contacted them. Now she keeps in touch intermittently. Her husband, who is taking steps to get a divorce, still doesn't know where she is.

Ellie is a runaway. Her mother died when she was young. Her father, a lawyer with a multinational oil company, never remarried. Ellie grew up with governesses and in boarding schools. She saw her father only on her school vacations and not always then. Soon after she turned fourteen, an event marked by a wire and a money order from her father, she longed desperately to see him. She was in school in Connecticut; he lived in Chicago. She couldn't reach him by phone, since he never returned her calls. Finally, driven by the fantasy that her father would embrace her and say, "Darling, I'm so glad to see you," she walked out of the school and bought an airplane ticket to Chicago. When she showed up at her father's office, though, it wasn't a pleased but an angry and impatient parent who greeted her. He called his secretary and had her put Ellie back on a plane bound for New York City. She was to alight at LaGuardia Airport and take a limousine to the Connecticut town closest to her school. She did get off at LaGuardia, but there her tracks ended. No one, not even the private detective hired by her father, could find her.

Sam is a runaway. Sam is seventy-five years old. The years have painfully caught up with him. His memory is failing, his powers of concentration are going, his bones ache. He finds the pace of life in a world that doesn't slow down for old people too dizzying for him. Still, at times flashes of a younger Sam — of a tough, resourceful, independent Sam — return. One time when this happened he felt a terribly urgent need to prove something to himself and to his oldest son, with whom he was living. "I didn't want 'em to write me off yet," he said later in a moment of lucidity. And so, cloudy of mind but clear of purpose, he took his entire savings — they amounted to $24 — from the cookie jar in which he'd kept them. Then Sam walked out of the house and made his way to the Greyhound bus depot. He bought a ticket to Philadelphia because his old wartime buddy, Tom, lived in Philadelphia. Tom would put him up. Would be fun to see that old son-of-a-gun again. For the moment Sam forgot that Tom had died four years before. Forgetting that fact didn't matter, anyway, for once he was in the bustling Philadelphia bus station the old man forgot why he was there at all. In fact, he wasn't sure where he was and stood there helpless until an alert Travelers Aid worker came to his rescue.

José is a runaway. Once this good-looking Puerto Rican, twenty-four years old, laughed at life; his was a macho kind of exuberance. But no more. He is one-armed now, in a world of impatient two-armed people. A grenade in Vietnam shredded that missing arm, and did away with a portion of his stomach, as well. Things were rough for José upon his return to his old haunts in East Harlem. He hurt physically. He was in pain mentally. He couldn't find a decent job. He saw himself as he assumed everybody else saw him — damaged goods, half a man. He was convinced his young wife stayed with him only out of pity; he imagined that his baby daughter, when she was older, would react to him with disdain. Heroin, with which he'd had some brief experience in Vietnam, beckoned. To support his habit he became a mugger. Rather than disgrace his little family, which he truly loves, José split. That was a year ago. And now? Now he stalks the streets, a violent man. He is also a runaway — a runaway who still dreams of returning to his wife and child someday.

José and Steve and Martha and Ellie and Sam — husbands, wives, children, aged persons — they are the runaways and there are more types still: former counterculture girls who try to lead the "straight" married life and find themselves straitjacketed by it. And persons who have escaped from mental institutions and nursing homes. And divorcing mothers and fathers, entangled in custody fights, who snatch up and run with the children who are the focus of the dispute.

Number as runaways, too, thousands upon thousands of men and women, solo travelers and pairs, pairs alone and with small children, wed and unwed — who aren't necessarily running from specific horror, who aren't necessarily running *to* anything in particular, either. Compulsion is what keeps them going: they live their lives devoid of an essential choice; they must run, must flee, must keep on the move. Akin to the hoboes of old, who used to ride the rails and warm a tin of beans over an open fire, they're floaters, drifters. They stay a few months here, a few months there. They push on aimlessly from city to city. They're often seen at Travelers Aid offices or bus station booths — broke, tired, hoping for a bed, a meal, maybe a job. But even if they get what they ask for, soon they're driven to move on again. Of all runaways, these people, with their irresistible urge to live their lives as fugitives, are the most unusual of all.

The Running is the Message

Floaters may be a puzzle, but husbands and wives who duck out on their spouses, and children who abandon their parents, are rather clearly defined in terms of conventional morality. Conventionally, they're immoral. They did wrong. They deserted. They quit and cut out — and in the most furtive, therefore wretched, way. Who respects a sneak? All right, if not sneaks, then — to be charitable — people who are rather unstable. Stable persons don't run away. We all have problems, some of us very serious ones. But we work on them, or make the best of things, or if we must get out we do so forthrightly.

But is that righteous view a truthful one in relation to the rest of us, who don't run away in the specific meaning of the term? If we're being utterly honest with ourselves we have to admit that we don't always face up to things, either. Each of us possesses emotional defense mechanisms — necessary armor for psychic survival. Armor in the form of rationalizing, denying reality, adopting patterns of avoidance. To avoid facing up to unpleasantnesses we sometimes "run" by losing ourselves in work, in lovers, in drink, in hobbies or in volunteer efforts. Runaways have also practiced some of these ways of dealing — or not dealing — with unhappy circumstances. But in time these no longer work. Then they get the jitters. And what is left? Where can they turn? So they run. Some become habituated to running whenever a new crisis occurs.

Running away is more than a desperate act, it is an existential statement. Like suicide. Running, with the exception of the few young kids who run as a lark, is always an expression of inner pain, inner turmoil. It is a way of saying, "I can't take it any more." Or, "I want out — at least for the moment." Or, "I need help." It is a way of saying, "Now you'll be sorry." Or, "This is the only way I can survive." Each runaway act doesn't necessarily embody all such messages, but most of the time a melange of motivations is involved when people run.

In the case of young people running away, the act is very often a sign of health. It is healthy for eleven-, twelve-, thirteen-, fourteen-, fifteen-year-olds to want a respite from destructive situations they feel they can't control or affect. In running they're not only abandoning their parents, often they're also abandoning their prescribed roles in scarring family dramas. Youth counselors say, "The kids who run often turn out to be the strongest members of their families. They're the only ones, at least, who are doing something to change things."

It can be said, in explaining why teenagers run, that indeed many have little power and very few options at home. What can you do if you're thirteen years old, for instance, and your father whips you with his belt whenever he gets drunk? But that doesn't hold true for adults. Adults have more power, more options, don't they? Theoretically, yes. But the power we adults hold and the options we have are far from immutable. Stress eats at us like a corrosive acid. The more stress we're under, the more conflict there is in our lives, the more confined and deprived and powerless we tend to feel. The more powerless we feel, the less capable we tend to be in exercising our options or even of perceiving them clearly. Think of a striking example: the abused wife whose husband beats and bruises and mauls her. Court papers don't lessen his violence and police reports don't diminish his danger. She feels she has no way out, either for herself or her children; for safety's sake, she has to run with them and hide.

But what about another kind of wife, the one whose husband never lays a hand on her but who feels emotionally battered because of his neglect of her? Can such an anguished and angry and utterly frustrated woman always deliberate rationally among the choices available to her? Many a woman can, of course. Yet some are stuck with just one panicky thought: "Got to get out. *Out.*"

Studies of earthquakes, tornadoes, floods, fires and other disasters show that the people who cope best with life-threatening situations are the ones best able to rationalize and intellectualize and marshal their inner resources on the spot. Instantly. Contrary to mass media reports, few people actually panic in disasters, but the ones who do tend to have certain personality traits in common: they're impulsive, easily angered, more sensitive to criticism; they tend to store up resentments instead of dealing with them directly, tend to have a hard time saying "no."

Even when it is premeditated rather than a more or less spur-of-the-moment act, running away most often is a panic reaction. People who look back on their runaway experiences often say something like, "I know it sounds silly now, but at the time it was the only thing I could think to do."

They say, "I was desperate."

It is the kind of desperation that leads some people, young and old, to commit suicide. In fact, running away can act as a safety valve that diminishes a desperate person's urge to kill himself or herself.

What emerges clearly is that people don't *choose* to run. They *need* to run. For those who need to run away, separation can serve as a time of rest, of healing — a calming time in which crashing waves of tension and bewilderment abate, and a little tranquillity returns to one's confused and agitated emotional life. A respite that, with luck, enables them to gain the strength to face their problems more directly and maturely. For some runaways, this is how it works out. For others it doesn't and, in one way or another, they never stop running.

Running away may not be the best answer to a problem, but at times it is the only answer.

Class Factors

Leah is forty-eight years old. She and her husband, a brick-layer, lived in the same house in northern New Jersey for twenty-six years. In that time Leah had four children and seven orgasms. Her husband told her he loved her once each year, on New Year's Eve, when he was very drunk. When he came home from work he expected dinner on the table — and got it. After dinner he drank beer and watched television; weekends he played softball or went hunting with his buddies. For a long time Leah saw herself as a widow and it was only shortly before her departure that she realized she was wishing her husband dead. She thought fleetingly about divorce. And quietly dismissed such heretical thoughts. Nobody in her family, in her crowd, did that; she couldn't see herself as she would become, the pariah of the neighborhood. So when her youngest child became a sophomore in high school she took the only alternative to divorce she could think of. Like a couple of other women in the same predicament whom she knew, Leah ran away.

Middle-class men and women, accustomed to easy treks to and from the divorce courts, may find it hard to believe that separation and divorce even now are still much more acceptable in their circles than in others. Yet, it is a fact. In working-class Catholic groups especially, divorce is still very much frowned upon. How do you shake off moral and religious scruples you began to absorb almost along with mother's milk? You don't. So what do you do when, in unhappy middle age, you can't eliminate them and can't go on living with your husband, either? You wait until your children are old enough and then you take off secretly, the first directly assertive move you've made for as long as you can remember.

In a respectable working-class section of Chelsea, in Manhattan, at least four such runaway wives are living within three blocks of each other. But though of similar backgrounds and in similar situations, they've never met — and the Italian matron who knows them all says they definitely don't want to identify themselves, not even to each other.

Desertion is, of course, a very common way of dissolving marriages among low-income persons. As long as lawyers charge hundreds of dollars to draw up the simplest of separation agreements that cost them less than $25 in filing and typing fees, and as long as Legal Aid lawyers are in short supply, legal separation and divorce are beyond the reach of a great many people. Besides, if you can't afford lawyers, how can you afford child support or, worse, alimony? So the thinking goes. So the desertions go.

Panicky Planners

Many persons who run don't seem to be running in panic. It may seem more calculating than panicky to run because you don't want to help pay your family's rent or food bills. It hardly seems to be panic running when you figure out ahead of time that Los Angeles is a good place to head for because the weather is warm and you might get into show biz. But panic running doesn't mean the act has to be precisely impulsive, exactly unplanned, as sudden and startling to the runaway as to the family members left behind. Some runaways go at it with the attitude, "I'm going to cover all contingencies." They plan and plan and plan. Sally was such a one. For months this runaway wife sent away for literature from hotels, motels and chambers of commerce in Atlanta,

Los Angeles, San Francisco, Miami, even San Juan. "If I was going to do it, I'd do it right, where I'd have the best chance of living cheaply and getting a job," she later said.

Peggy, another careful planner, counted days and dollars, parlaying her bowling winnings to $1,000 — at which point she'd reached her target and took off. Sal, a runaway husband who worked in a sporting goods store, told all of his co-workers, who were sympathetic to him, that he was going to run from home. "Don't say anything to anyone who might ask about me when I've split," he warned them. He was meticulous about covering his tracks.

Other people, other temperaments. We're all of a piece; people who are generally impulsive won't suddenly plan their runaway episodes with the dedicated patience of a chess strategist. Some people are obsessed with the thought of leaving, yet plan so poorly they wind up in strange cities without knowing where to go and what to do. For instance, a social worker in the Travelers Aid office in downtown Los Angeles says, "We see a number of runaway wives who end up in Hollywood drawn by the glamour of the place. They have the movie-star syndrome. They feel twenty-five dollars should do them until the first paycheck, but they don't even have a job."

In one sense, though, everyone is a planner — in the sense of preparing mentally for the fact of taking off. Genuinely spontaneous running is very unusual. "In all of my runaway cases the spouses have been thinking about it an awful lot, thinking about just leaving the whole thing," is how a case-worker at the Family Service of Los Angeles puts it.

Among juvenile runaways as among adult ones there are the methodical planners and the ones who take off with little forethought. Teenagers usually don't have the financial resources available to some adult runaways, but frequently there is a counterbalancing factor at work on their behalf — an informal runaway network. So many adolescents have run, and spread the word to other teens, that at least some of those who want to take off can do so with the certainty that they will be taken care of, at least during their initial days away. A fifteen-year-old girl who threatened to run away told her mother with startling assurance, "I know exactly where I'll go and who'll help me." And, indeed, when she actually did take off for almost a week it was a network of friends and acquaintances who helped her.

Referring to the juvenile runaways he has encountered, Ron Johnson of the Family and Children's Service of Minneapolis, says, "They check things out first, make contacts, do some planning — more than some adults."

Warning Signals

However they arrange their escapes, whether haphazardly or with the kind of skill and cleverness Machiavelli would have admired, runaways of all kinds signal their intent to go. They may not say a word, but they send forth the signal that a runaway episode is in the offing. The signs are there. For the runaway's family the problem lies in being able — or wanting — to spot them.

The most telling sign, the overriding pattern that precedes a runaway episode, is behavioral change. The change may be as obvious as the one in which a husband who used to consume two martinis a night now consumes five. The change may be as subtle as the one in which a wife who had an occasional headache now gets them several times a week. Frequently runaways start to run for some time before actually disappearing. Theirs are trial runs, so to speak.

"One thing I noticed, John would come home later and later; he'd find things to take him out of the house," recalls a wife whose mate skipped out on her, leaving behind two children and a ransacked savings account. Like husbands, like wives. They, too, discover all kinds of ways, real or invented, for plausibly being away from a home that no longer feels like home to them — clubs, volunteer efforts, the bowling league, the night out with the girls . . . Not that everyone who leads a seemingly busy life is a potential runaway. But when people make new or newly vigorous efforts to absent themselves from their families, it frequently does tend to be a sign that something is seriously wrong.

Potential runaways often complain. They're dissatisfied. Disillusioned. Frustrated. One way or another they may say, "You're not listening to me!" Withdrawal — sexual, emotional or both — characterizes the actions of a great many spouses who run. As a left-behind wife sadly remarked, "Toward the end we never talked any more, never touched any more, never did things together any more."

She sounded like a woman whose marriage is on the verge of cracking up. And it is obviously true that all of the symptoms of marital ills that precede separation or divorce can also antecede a runaway act.

Youthful runaways, too, throw out clues as to their growing tension, frustration and unhappiness. Young people signal their plight by changes in their customary ways of behaving. The talkative youth becomes quiet and withdrawn. The youth who has never, or only minimally, experimented with drugs now becomes a heavy drug or alcohol user. The hitherto well-behaved boy or girl becomes rude, sullen, angrily rebellious; the generally more rebellious one becomes a serious behavior problem. There may be constant parent-child hassles over rules, restrictions, chores, appearance. Because so much of the teenager's life is taken up with school work, it stands to reason that incipient runaways undergo dramatic changes in their functioning in this area of their lives. They become lax in doing their homework. They lose interest in studying. They act up in classes and cut school. Their grades plummet.

Like adult runaways-in-the-making, juvenile ones also often "practice" for their eventual taking off, by such acts as staying out later and later (ignoring parent-imposed curfews), and spending nights at friends' homes but "forgetting" to tell their parents where they are. This behavior tends to accelerate, to become a patterned way of handling tensions at home. It may finally lead to an actual runaway episode.

Revealing as warning signals are, they obviously should not be seen as unfailing predictors of a runaway act. First, it is a combination of such signs that more accurately reflects the extreme unhappiness or discontent that prompts someone to run away. Second, many youths (and adults) display these symptoms without actually leaving — though this fact doesn't lessen their meaning as indicators of distress. Third, behavioral changes of the kind described here needn't be dramatic. As Dr. James S. Gordon of the National Institute of Mental Health (NIMH) explains, "Parents often say a kid's getting worse, but it may be more a matter of degree than of startling change. Parents may say the behavior is suddenly going on, when in fact it has been going on for a while and they haven't noticed."

All in all it becomes clear that the people who run — *those* husbands, *those* wives, *those* parents, *those* children — really aren't so different from the rest of us. Their stresses are, after all, familiar ones. To a greater or lesser degree we also know the unfortunate financial or family circumstances in which they're entangled — if not at firsthand, luckily, then because they've occurred to someone close to us.

Learning more about the people who feel compelled to leave their surroundings in such an unorthodox manner, and about the spouses or parents or children they left behind, may illuminate aspects of our own lives and the lives of persons dear to us. Learning how best to cope with abandonment — and with the reunion that often follows abandonment — may give us insights into better ways of coping with other traumatic and disturbing family experiences. We are them and they are us.

2

Yesterday's Runaways:
Following An
American Tradition

Runaways Everywhere

They've always been among us here, everywhere. There isn't a country that does not have its runaways. In 1956 the United Nations dealt with the problem of deserting husbands by creating mechanisms by which a wife in one country, whose husband deserted to another, nevertheless could make her claim for support and, if necessary, file suit.

Countries where emigration and immigration were in flux — Germany and Japan, for example — were most eager to sign such a compact. The United States wasn't even represented. The Scandinavian countries could be pardoned for having a feeling of déjà vu: they'd had a reciprocal agreement of this kind among them since 1931.

In 1971 the British journal *The Economist* reported on the existence of "several hundred thousand" deserted wives whose husbands weren't helping to support them; most were receiving supplementary benefits from the government's Department of Health and Social Security.

A Soviet journalist, writing in Moscow's *Literaturnaya Gazeta* in the mid-1960s, described teenage runaways in the Soviet Union. An *Atlas* magazine translation of the article states that some of these youths had run as many as eleven times, some were on the road for three months before being caught by the authorities. Regardless of how brutal their home circumstances may have been — and in some cases it was very brutal — they were arrested, detained, and finally sent home.

Early American Runaways

Runaways are very much a part of American history, as they are of Russian history. Some of the early colonial adventurers were runaways. Then as now, financial woes were a primary reason for leaving home and hearth and setting out for the great unknown. This was England's condition in the early 1600s: severe economic depression, mass hunger, political strife, religious persecution. Many men and some women decided to flee the misery. Between 1607 and 1642 some 70,000 of them left. Many headed for the West Indies, some for New England.

As the colonies became settled, more conventional deserters emerged. Just as the Babylonian king Hammurabi had to deal with the runaway husband in his domain over thirty-seven hundred years ago — he did so by ruling that a deserted wife might remarry — so, as early as 1685, the colony of Rhode Island had to deal with the deserting family man. Like other runaway husbands, the Rhode Island ones were fed up with their lot, bored by their wives, drawn by adventure. But they left their families behind without support, and Rhode Island decided to help. It was a significant step, in terms of a colonial government's acknowledgment of the problem and its willingness to do something about it.

America opened up. The great westward migration began. For many hardworking men, tired of scrabbling endlessly for a meager living in a restrictive society, the chance to head for the unknown, and probably do better financially than they had been doing, maybe even strike it rich, became irresistible. With or without their families they went. Mobility became the keynote of progress. All ambitious men were prompted by the same motto: "Move onward and climb upward." They became migrants again. Some migrants were runaways, many were not. The crucial element is that the westward migration crystallized something in the American spirit: *Stand still and rot; pack your belongings, head out and you'll win.*

Wanderlust

Writing about the significance of the frontier, the great historian Frederic Jackson Turner suggested that migration provided some psychological releases for the men and women who migrated westward. Release from what? Maybe closeness. Maybe permanent social ties. They crossed the newly carved passes, they traversed the already famous trails like the Oregon and the Santa Fe, they met and made new friends. And they moved on, leaving these new friends behind.

But it wasn't only the western frontier that beckoned. As always, some men simply ran away from home — to travel westward or just to travel, as long as they were putting distance between themselves and their families. By now, though, the runaway fever had struck a growing number of wives as well. There were enough of them, at any rate, for newspapers of the day to carry ads placed by the angry husbands left behind. Consider this choice and revealing item from an issue of the *South Carolina Gazette* in 1764:

"LYDIA, The wife of John Wilson, having eloped from her husband, he hereby forbids all Persons to give her any credit in his name, being determined not to pay any debt of her contracting, from this 28th day of October 1764. He likewise forbids the harbouring or entertaining his said wife, on pain of prosecution."

It's clear that "eloping" in those days was a common synonym for "running away." It's also clear that the ideals later proposed by the Declaration of Independence weren't being enthusiastically extended to the female sex in that era. On the contrary. American legal practice, based on English common law, held that married women couldn't hold title to property in their own names; moreover, they were legally subject to their husbands. That, of course, didn't prevent individual women from liberating themselves insofar as they could. Bold Sarah Cantwell, who placed the following saucy ad in the *South Carolina and American Gazette* in 1776, was obviously a model of the liberated woman of her time:

"John CANTWELL has the Impudence to advertise me in the Papers, cautioning all Persons against crediting me; he never had any Credit till he married me: As for his Bed and Board he mentioned, he had neither Bed nor Board when he married me; I never eloped, I went away before his Face when he beat me."

Runaway Slaves

"It was an old plantation maxim, 'Never threaten a Negro or he will run,'" notes Samuel Eliot Morison in *The Oxford History of the American People*. Plantation owners were obsessed with the fear that their two-legged properties might run, and became enraged when they did. When those escaping blacks ran from south to north via the "underground railways" of the day, they were housed and fed by sympathizers — much as runaway teenagers, crisscrossing the country, are today.

The Immigrant Wave

Shortly after the turn of this century, as wave after wave of Jews from eastern and southern Europe, Greeks, Sicilians and Slavs washed up on our not always so welcoming shores, a new type of runaway emerged — the immigrant runaway. More than a million of them fled their homelands annually during many of the years in the 1905–1914 period.

They came here as runaways from persecution and poverty. They arrived heady with fantasies about the fabled New World. They looked for the gold-paved streets. They discovered garbage and sweatshops and cramped tenements.

Was this what they had fled the Old Country for? Were they expected to slave on endlessly to put a little chicken soup into their families' bellies? Life must be better elsewhere in this great nation, they thought, so many of them ran away to find that better life. Jewish husbands and fathers especially, their ambitions stifled, their vistas shrunk, finally felt compelled to flee.

Actually, there were two types of runaway husbands. The first type told his wife in the *stetl,* "I'll go to New York, get a good job, and as soon as I've got a few dollars saved up I'll send for you and the children." But he never got around to sending for her — either because he never could save up those few dollars or, just as likely, because he found the sophisticated Jewish girls in New York City far more appealing than the peasant wife he left behind. The second type of runaway husband did bring his family over, or acquired one here, but finally the grinding poverty to which he was endlessly subjected got the better of him. And, after a period of boozing or womanizing, he split.

No attempt was made to understand the social and psychological processes whereby a timid *stetl* soul, brought up to show reverence for the family, could become a family deserter. "Unfortunately, there is nothing so common today in our large cities as family desertion and non-support — and the misery of it all is that it is caused not so much by lack of work or other economic reasons as by addiction to drink, fickleness and infidelity, and a moral obtuseness to the parents' duty to the children," thundered one righteous judge, William H. DeLacy of Washington, D.C., in 1910. Some other critics were even sterner: their censure contained a whiff of anti-immigrant sentiment.

The Jewish philanthropies, too, were becoming edgy. They talked about the plight of the poor wives and children left behind by these irresponsible men, but their concern was also rooted in practicalities. Deserted families are often left destitute and somebody must pay for the roof over their heads and the bread that goes into their mouths. That means city departments, philanthropic agencies. How long can these pay and pay without taking drastic action? In 1909 a principal Jewish charity, the United Hebrew Charities of New York, did take drastic action. It established a separate section whose sole function was dealing with desertion cases — not only in providing relief for abandoned families, but also in finding and prosecuting the men who abandoned them. It was a first in the charity field.

A first or not, the tide of Jewish immigrant runaway husbands showed no signs of abating, so two years later this section was phased out. It was replaced by the establishment of a whole organization dedicated only to the proposition that runaway husbands must be found, returned to the fold or prosecuted, and made to pay their dues. Named the National Desertion Bureau, it was unique to the United States and, probably, to the world; it still survives as the Family Location and Legal Services. More about FLS later in the book.

The National Desertion Bureau was both ingenious and efficient. Swiftly it wove together a worldwide network of cooperating social agencies whose sole function it was to ferret out information about each deserter in question —

from his relatives, friends and fellow employees. The bureau was also adept at using newspapers to further its purposes: it got Jewish papers in New York City, Chicago, Montreal and Toronto to publish on a regular basis a rogues' gallery of missing husbands, complete with photos and descriptions. These features paid off; over the years readers saw the photos, recognized them — "That looks like Yankl, the man with the shifty eyes, who rooms next door" — and became informers.

Not every escapee husband who was finally collared returned to the family nest. Some refused to come home but bowed to the pressure to make support payments. A handful of stubborn men refused to do anything at all. Consider the remarkable case of Elias Zepnick, whose story occupied the pages of the charities journal *Survey* in April 1913. Zepnick had deserted his wife Yetta and their eight young children, leaving them penniless in New York. A few years later he was finally tracked down in St. Louis. Confronted there, he shocked officials by refusing to cooperate with them in any way.

They'd never come across such an obstinate man before! The Legal Aid Bureau went to work, bringing proceedings under a new child abandonment law that made it a felony in New York City to abandon one's children and leave them destitute. Zepnick was arrested and extradited to New York.

Then, practically at the point of sentencing, the court made an astounding discovery. Zepnick was wealthy — he had $790 stashed away in a St. Louis bank! The judge pleaded with the errant husband to provide for his family, holding out the carrot of a suspended sentence if he now acted responsibly. We can only guess why Elias Zepnick refused. Was he so bitter toward Yetta for whatever reason? Was he too proud to change his mind? At any rate, his stand got him two years' hard labor at Sing Sing and a $1,000 fine. While in prison he made repeated applications to be released — yet, when asked, always refused to release the money in his bank account. Finally he lost it anyway, as a result of a civil action. Eventually he was released.

Survey concluded, "Some little redress has been secured and now the Zepnick family will be able to enjoy a legitimate gratuity. Zepnick himself, however, is still obdurate and is believed to be in London and thus beyond the jurisdiction of our courts."

Not that the immigrant runaway problem was solely a Jewish problem. Irish immigrants also deserted their families. So did Greeks and Slavs. But they were fewer in number and their departures weren't so well publicized. Many more simply abandoned wives and children by leaving them behind in Europe, and forgetting about them once they got here. A fairly typical incident: In 1908 a Glasgow agency advanced transportation to men willing to work on a huge Canadian railway project; within five years 340 families had been deserted and were seeking relief from their local parish. Glasgow officials sought to counter the trend by allowing married men to emigrate only if they reported regularly to some duly constituted authority in Canada, and by making immediate deportation the consequence of desertion.

Depression Nomads

From the early years of this century well into the twenties, the runaway problem consisted in the main of runaway husbands. The Depression changed all that, however. Hunger became the great equalizer. Being the hobo, the vagabond, the deserter was no longer an adult male prerogative. More women ran. And hordes of teenagers of both sexes roamed the country, looking for work, for fun, for something to replace the despairing atmosphere of want at home. This, too, was new and striking. Of course boys and girls (mostly boys) had run away from home before — and Mark Twain's *The Adventures of Huckleberry Finn,* published in 1884, romanticized them. Nevertheless, they weren't all that attention-getting; up to the Depression era hardly anything with respect to juvenile runaways had been noted in the appropriate literature, either professional or popular.

During the Depression years of 1932 and 1933 especially, boys and girls left home in great numbers. They lived in boxcars. They camped in hobo jungles on the edge of towns. They stayed in caves and warehouses and deserted buildings. Some of the girls traveled in pairs, some with their boyfriends, some in gangs of a dozen or so.

Thomas Minehan, a writer who spent some time on the road with these prowling teenagers, observed that in the Depression's early days few boy "tramps" and virtually no girls were visible on the road. As the economy worsened and home conditions became increasingly intolerable, boys of high school age and younger popped up in unfamiliar places, looking for work. Girls were the last to appear — at first hitchhiking from one resort to another, looking for work. As with the boys, older girls came first; the younger ones who followed them passed up the resorts and headed for the railroads; not coincidentally, that's where the boys were. Division of labor was what it is today in urban youth gangs — the girls cooked for the boys, served the boys, had sex with them; in return they got what they seemingly wanted and needed — companionship and protection.

Initially, according to Minehan, the wandering teenagers came from "laboring homes of little culture." By 1934, though, plenty of boys and girls from "good homes" were represented.

At the height of the Depression the Transient Emergency Act provided federal funds for states to set up transient detention camps; the teenagers shunned these camps at all costs. For a while, to avoid being caught, they stopped traveling in packs. Then, having acquired greater sophistication, many learned how to travel together without facing legal action. But they were less successful in getting relief dollars in strange towns. Generally, both juveniles and adults met the same fate when they turned up in a new city: relief authorities gave them exactly one day to get out of town.

Runaway War Babies

So much for the first wave of teenage transients to cross and crisscross the country. A second manifested itself in the patriotic early 1940s, following hard on the heels of Pearl Harbor. Most working-age men were gone, conscripted into the service; women and teenagers of both sexes flocked to the mushrooming war plants to sign up for good jobs. Again, there was a rhythm to the peregrinations of the young; sixteen- and seventeen-year-olds left home first to take jobs in other states; inevitably, their juniors followed soon after. Some of the younger ones pretended to be older.

The *Annals of the American Academy of Political and Social Science* thought the situation serious enough to publish in November 1944 an article entitled "Adolescents Away From Home." It described "boys and girls — many not yet in their teens, who have left home without the permission of their parents or guardians to seek excitement and high adventure or to escape from unhappiness in home and community."

The authors of the article (both associated with the Children's Bureau) pointed out that funds generally weren't available to send these runaway youths back to their home communities. So what happened to them? Often they were simply turned loose at the borders of the county where they were caught — or given just enough money to get them out of that jurisdiction. "Let somebody else take responsibility for them" became the humane watchword of the day.

As for the older teenagers, the young migrants who found

jobs in wartime industries far from home, nobody really gave a damn about them, either. They remained unsupervised. Housing shortages forced many to live in flophouses and cheap hotels. Recreational activities? Nonexistent.

In fact, the runaway youth was no longer the romantic figure he had been in myth and literature. Huckleberry Finn had become an anachronism. Resented by the communities where they sought jobs, teenage migrants and runaways became dubious characters in the public's practical mind. The Children's Bureau specialists who wrote the *Annals* article made some radical proposals: provide shelter for the younger runaways, counseling and recreational activities for all of them, treat them as children and adolescents whose running away is a symptom of unhappiness and maladjustment.

Generally in the public's mind, however, that was a lot of psychological claptrap. Unhappiness? Maladjustment? Runaways were lawbreakers, pure and simple — juvenile delinquents who'd grow up to be adult criminals if they were mollycoddled. *That* was the prevailing tone of the time.

Postwar Deserters

In the wake of World War II the nation experienced another minor upsurge in runaway husbands. These were, for the most part, veterans. They had married just before going off to boot camp or right after coming home, and now were bored with their conventional lives — or bored with what they saw as so conventional. The surge of male immigrant deserters had been looked upon askance both for economic and moral reasons; the postwar crop of deserting husbands received sympathy. These were pre-Women's Liberation years, after all, and the ethos of the times was that if a husband wasn't happy his wife was doing something wrong.

It was right in keeping with "togetherness" and other such concepts the women's magazines were promoting. So it was that an article on deserting husbands, in the October 1950 issue of *Good Housekeeping*, pinpointed the main reason why many a husband fled from his home. His wife. She was at fault. She'd failed to make her mate "feel he is the center of her own particular universe . . . failed in the biggest job a woman can accept."

The article was written by a woman.

The Counterculture Wave

So we come to the latest great migratory wave, the counter-culture youth movement — a movement in all senses of the term — of the late 1960s and early 1970s. That era has already been relegated to nostalgia. But recall. The Vietnam War, the overriding cause of the day, embodied all of the resentments of young people: helplessness in the face of adult authority, bitterness against parents, revulsion against materialism, hatred of the war itself and of their own potential involvement in it. There was heady, idealistic talk — and talk and talk — of changing the system, remaking the society, smashing down injustices. There were causes galore correlating with Vietnam: civil rights and the Indians and poisons in our food and pollution of the atmosphere. There was the New Left and the New New Left as political splintering inevitably occurred; there were the marches on Washington and the demonstrations — all those demonstrations at political conventions, on college campuses, in some of the high schools. And there were the Beatles and the rock concerts — rock being the symbol of the new liberation and solidarity of the young.

It was a symbol, too, of their idealization and exploitation. The sixties saw a kind of worshiping of youth — and, consequently, a hating of them, as well — unmatched even in this youth-worshiping nation. Most of all the sixties saw a breaking down of the isolation of the young as teenagers throughout the country, throughout the world, suddenly became brothers and sisters, finding a marvelous instant identification with each other. And "make love not war," and grass, and acid, and acid rock, and pop festivals were the hub around which this occurred.

But what has all this to do with runaways? It was the festivals, beginning with the Monterey Pop Festival of 1966, that activated the counterculture runaway explosion. The festivals were the Pied Piper, luring kids by the thousands, by the hundreds of thousands, to the grassy open spaces far, far from home.

The festivals drew them first, but quickly they dispersed to other meccas, to communities already become or becoming refuges for the alienated, communities studded with crash pads and communes, those hippie homesteads — Hollywood and Venice in the Los Angeles area, Haight-Ashbury in San Francisco, Telegraph Avenue in Berkeley, Boston's South End, Georgetown and Dupont Circle in Washington, D.C., the East Village in Manhattan — those were the magic names.

Both hippies and runaways, and runaways-become-hippies, presented serious problems for themselves and for the communities that unwillingly played host to them. Medical problems. Psychological problems. Problems having to do with the fact that the kids were broke, hungry and lost. There were bad trips, drug-connected hepatitis, VD, unwanted pregnancies, upper respiratory infections, urinary and genital tract infections brought on by poor living conditions and neglect — in some cases long-standing neglect because alienated youths wouldn't see establishment physicians (who didn't want much to do with them, either). So it was that the sixties saw the advent of free clinics in Haight-Ashbury, Los Angeles and elsewhere, started by socially conscious young doctors and other volunteers. The first runaway houses were as informally begun at roughly the same time.

In some circles it's the custom nowadays to romanticize the young of the sixties, not only the college-age hippies but the hordes of much younger runaways, too. The romanticizers say they ran only for the music, the kicks, the experience — or to make a statement protesting an amoral society as represented by their restrictive families of origin. (Well, yes, they'd acknowledge, maybe there was a little old-fashioned rebelliousness at work there, too.)

At best, this is a simplistic view. Unarguably, some kids had a strong political consciousness (though their impact was out of all proportion to their numbers). Certainly some kids ran for the excitement. A New York City College student, himself a former runaway who "crashed" — that is, found shelter with friends and strangers — in the East Village, recalls, "All these thirteen-year-olds, these girls, would get on the bus and come to New York. They were going to find love and happiness in the East Village, and a lot of them got right back on the bus and went home."

But many, many of the young runaways then, as before and now, had serious personal problems. Many came from conflict-ridden, even pathological, homes. "A lot of the kids had pretty rough family scenes," says the NIMH's Dr. James Gordon, who lived in Haight-Ashbury at the time.

Then, however, few people — including mental health professionals and youth workers — were aware of that. Runaways were more adept at talking about drugs and politics, at ripping apart the Great Robot Society, than at revealing themselves as persons who hurt. "Everything's cool, man, make love, you know?" That was the approach which established instant camaraderie. And the professionals were not yet looking closely at what was going on in the runaways' families.

Thus the myth of the counterculture runaways as social or political adventurers, if not just as happy-go-lucky kids, came into being. But even without a lot of probing it should have been self-evident that something was radically amiss with these young flower children blown hither and yon. They were so intent on establishing their own peer-level families, their own little nourishing communities. Had they had enough of that kind of thing at home, would they really have been searching for it so desperately elsewhere? It took a long time for people to listen, to realize that there was more going on at home than hassles about hair and clothes.

PART TWO:

The Children

3

Runaway Adolescents: A Runaway Problem

How Many?

One million — now, there's a striking figure. It keeps turning up in congressional hearings and elsewhere; it is supposed to represent the number of boys and girls in the United States who run away each year. Its origins are murky. It's meant to be an extrapolation of some FBI statistics, questionably accurate to begin with, on juvenile runaways. But it has been politically useful in dramatizing the seriousness of the runaway problem and in drumming up congressional support for federal funding of runaway programs. One study sponsored by the federal government puts the annual runaway minors figure at around 300,000. Still another study, compiled in 1975 by the National Center for Health Statistics, showed that one youth in ten from the ages of twelve to seventeen had run away from home at some point.

That still seems like a lot. In any event, for the kids who get into trouble as a result of their runaway episodes, and for the anguished parents who wait by the phone hoping for some word from them, the figures are irrelevant. If it's your own son or daughter out there, one runaway is plenty.

Who Runs?

In terms of economic and family background, nobody's child is exempt. There's the executive's fifteen-year-old son in Scarsdale, New York, who can no longer stand the way his parents complain about his use of drugs and choice of friends. There's the Pennsylvania steelworker's daughter who runs to escape her father's rage — rage at her boyfriend, who's black. There's the Minneapolis shopkeeper's daughter, two months pregnant and afraid to tell her folks. There's the ghetto youth whose father, in drunken fury, whips him with an electric cord. There's the Los Angeles girl whose father, a television producer, attempts to molest her when he drinks too much.

And then there are the kids here, there, everywhere, who have tremendous fights with their parents about such things as clothes or length of hair. And the ones who are scared witless by the bad grades they're getting, and run impulsively.

Only three things do they all have in common: they're young, they're runaways, and they hurt.

South Boston Runaways

What happened in South Boston during its violent antibusing days of the middle 1970s is depressingly instructive. It shows how even when everything at home seems peaceful on the surface, parents can unwittingly create a situation that results in their children's running. Countless Irish and Italian parents in the neighborhood told their kids not to attend school with the bused-in blacks. Time on their hands, bored, the white students ended up on the Boston Common where, for the first time, they met up with the runaways and the street kids hanging out there. They were fascinated by them.

And why not? This was a study in contrasts. The South Boston youngsters' home life was rigid, their backgrounds law-and-order; they lived in public housing pockets, many of them, and hadn't really known Boston as a big city. When their parents' anti-busing stance led them out of South Boston they encountered kids who laughed at law-and-order, at parental rules; kids who smoked grass in public and scoffed at curfews; kids who had "freedom."

Sister Barbara Whalen, who heads a Boston runaway house, The Bridge, Inc., tells how the South Boston teenagers distanced themselves from their parents. First they hung out on the Boston Common or in Harvard Square — thirteen-, fourteen-year-olds getting to know seventeen-, eighteen-year-olds. They started to drink a little. They began sleeping around, getting into the drug scene; for some this served as a springboard for dealing and prostitution.

It was a step-by-step process for these South Boston kids, Sister Barbara says. "You could see them gradually enjoying the streets. They loved the freedom — they were out there from ten in the morning to eleven at night with no one telling them what to do."

More and more they were drawn to the streets. And, in a number of cases, the streets claimed them; they no longer wanted to go home.

Runaways vs. Throwaways

In a sense all runaways are "throwaways," pushed out of their homes or institutions by circumstances or people they can no longer cope with. But the term "throwaways" has come specifically to mean a fairly new phenomenon — kids who have become urban nomads. They're mostly black and Hispanic. They come from low-income families and their folks, to ease their financial pressures or for other reasons, have literally pushed them out of their homes. As a caseworker at The Door, which describes itself as a "center of alternatives" for adolescents in Manhattan, put it, "Some parents are no longer considering a sixteen-year-old kid a kid. They're being forced to grow up and take care of themselves."

A number of these boys and girls live in foster homes on and off. In New York City alone there may be several hundred thousand of them, homeless kids roaming the streets, living on rooftops or in abandoned buildings. Their needs are massive — medical, dental, emotional, legal, educational; they need job training; they need *everything*.

In New York City some runaway shelters have shifted their orientation from runaways to throwaways. Their reasoning is that runaways at least have homes they can go back to. Throwaways have nothing. The truth is that both groups need help; it's the scarcity of funding to help young people that forces such an "either-or" attitude.

When Do Runaways Run? From Where?

South Boston and throwaways aside, peak runaway times would coincide with the first hot week of spring; just after school closed in the summer; September (when schools opened again and kids were hit with the pressure to perform); at the time the first report cards of the year were issued; after the Christmas holidays (when teenagers, like adults, fall victim to the post-holiday blues).

While these patterns still hold to some extent, they aren't as predictable as they used to be. Sister Barbara offers an explanation that has an ominous ring to it: "Kids are more prone now to go *whenever* the pressure's on, they're not worrying about whether it's spring or warm or what."

During the height of the counterculture era runaway boys and girls used to travel great distances — from New York to the Midwest, then on to the West Coast; from California to Florida, then to New York; from Boston to Florida to . . . To wherever was far, the farther the better.

That's no longer true, at least not among the runaways who bed down in runaway houses. There out-of-staters are in the minority now. What has happened is that runaways generally stick closer to home. Drivers' fear of being robbed makes it much harder to thumb rides than it used to be. Also, more kids from working-class and low-income backgrounds are splitting, and they're less used to long-distance travel.

Vital Statistics

As in the Depression years, the runaways who ran a few years ago were in their middle and late teens; then the younger ones followed. Now fourteen- to sixteen-year-old runaways are common and the age is dropping. A Metropolitan Washington Council of Governments study on runaway youths in the Washington area reports that a growing number of runaways are in the eleven-to-thirteen-year-old bracket.

More girls than boys run — or so it seems. (Boys aren't as likely to show up at runaway shelters, nor are parents of boys as likely to report them missing.) Yet more boys do bed down in shelters than in the past, probably reflecting the difficulty they have in making it on the streets. Girls are more prone than boys to buddy up — either to run away accompanied by girlfriends or boyfriends or to team up with someone on the road. Many runaway counselors say there is less use of hard drugs now than there was a few years ago. Most no longer count pot smoking as "drug use."

Several studies show the same thing: many runaway youths stay away only a day or two or three. Most return home within a week. On the other hand, the longer a youth is on the road, the greater the chance that he won't return home. The more often a youth runs, the longer he's apt to stay away each successive time. Eventually many chronic runaways, repeaters, remain away forever.

The Friendship Network

However long a teenager stays away — days, weeks, months years — the name of the game is survival. You've got to eat. You've got to have someplace to sleep. You've got to make connections. You've got to depend on the goodwill of friends or strangers.

Friends. Of all the people and places that runaways can turn to for help, it's their friends they turn to the most. The majority of runaway kids use friends' homes as runaway "shelters." And what do the parents of the kids who provide the shelters have to say about that? Often, not a thing. The reason: they don't know what is going on.

"Look at the kinds of homes the kids live in," Sister Marlene Barghini, director of The Bridge for Runaway Youth, a shelter in Minneapolis, points out. "There are split-levels, upstairs, downstairs, basements — often parents don't even know what kids are there."

Split-levels belong to the middle class. But things are no different in many low-income neighborhoods. Often those tenement pads are crowded with people, with friends coming in and out; how are parents to know who belongs and who doesn't?

Runaway teens and their friends are clever. They're collusive: the runaway sneaks in at night, when the host's parents are asleep, sneaks out again at dawn, before they wake up. According to Mike, a sixteen-year-old in suburban Chicago whose friends have put him up on three separate occasions, "It's okay if you want to cool off for a couple of days." Mike did; he needed to. Each one of his disappearances followed a bitter fight between himself and his parents.

A couple of days, a couple of weeks — and more. The arrangement can be stretched out over time, given a well-knit group of cooperating friends. What they set up is an arrangement akin to an underground railway. The fleeing teenager is handed from friend to friend to friend, surreptitiously staying with each for short periods of time.

Incredibly, a minority of popular and cunning runaways makes a career of the underground rotation life. Al is one such. Shortly after his fourteenth birthday he was almost constantly away from home, yet never more than a mile from it. He had loads of friends and managed to spend as long as three months at a clip with some of them. A few of the parents knew he was staying with them — he'd turn up for dinner from time to time — but because he was very likable and helpful they tolerated his presence. The summer months were his biggest problem; most of his friends and their families were away then. So he would spend some of those warm nights huddled on top of staircases in apartment buildings. At seventeen Al grew tired of running and his parents grew tired of fighting him. They reconciled and he returned home to live.

There are variations on the theme. In Riverdale, a solidly middle-class enclave of New York City, runaway youths have taken advantage of warm spring and summer nights to sleep in the local park, showering and eating at friends' houses.

Somewhere on the wide open spaces that mark one of the less populated sections of the San Fernando Valley, in Los Angeles, is a rather remarkable variation. It consists of closed clubs, cultures, societies, each composed of from three to fourteen middle-teenagers. These kids don't hang out in shopping malls or at each other's houses; they don't need to, for they've gouged out a series of underground forts.

Those forts are carpeted, lit by candles and lanterns, furnished with couches, tables, stereos and other items they've ripped off somewhere. According to a youth worker in the area, when these teenagers want to disappear for a while, that's where they go. Weekend evenings, that's where they go. Parents know the forts exist, he says, but don't know where. The only kids caught are those working on their forts when the police helicopter goes by. Girls aren't allowed to be members, but girlfriends are brought in. Everyone is sworn to secrecy. This is a unique exurban analogue to inner-city youth gangs. The youth worker, who was taken down to one of the forts, describes it as made up of a central room from which several tunnels shoot out, emptying into other rooms. "It was," he says, "the most incredible thing I've ever seen."

Against the Law

To understand the life of the underage runaway requires an understanding of the legal rights of minors generally. To put it bluntly: at best minors are second-class citizens, lacking many of the rights, rights conducive to survival, that adults have. They can't work legally without work permits, which parents or guardians must approve. Some school districts won't allow minors to enroll without parental or guardian sponsorship. In most states physicians are reluctant to treat unattended minors for general medical problems — especially minors under fifteen — because of legal risks involved when parental approval isn't forthcoming. The under-eighteen age group has trouble renting rooms, even when the rent is paid in advance; hotels and rooming houses are leery of "wild" adolescents and don't want to be accused of harboring runaways. As for driver's licenses, even if the minimum driving age is sixteen, most states require parental permission. A recent study, *The Legal Status of Runaway Children,* points out that some restrictions "seem more in the nature of curfews imposed upon minors because they are minors, without regard to their driving records." As for curfews imposed on minors, numerous states and countless localities have them on their books, effectively controlling the movement of minors where they are enforced.

A philosophical debate about the necessity, morality and effectiveness of these and many other restrictions and limitations on the lives of minors is beyond this book's scope. But it has to be stated that the labyrinth of laws through which minors must thread their way until they reach the age of majority does carry with it significant implications. Minor-age persons are literally in bondage — to their parents and, through their parents, to society as a whole. Presumably the aim of the restrictions is threefold: (1) to protect teenagers from themselves; (2) to protect them from others; (3) to protect others from them. But they do seem to be weighted in the last direction — as if we're afraid of our teenagers and must shackle them with all kinds of legal limitations or they'll be monsters run amok.

Some controls are obviously needed, on adolescents as on adults; the preservation of society demands it, something that keeps eluding the more fanatical advocates of permissiveness. Too, all the evidence keeps pointing to the fact that younger adolescents especially need help with their "crazy" impulses, need some limits set on their behavior, both at home and in the community. But there are still questions of kind and degree and appropriateness worth considering.

Another consideration is the attitude toward "authority figures" — mothers and fathers and teachers and police and others — engendered in teenagers who keep getting the message that they're owned and feared. It is hard to imagine how, under the circumstances, an atmosphere of mutual respect, mutual recognition of each other's right to autonomy, can exist in the parent-child relationship, especially in the case of children who aren't by nature tractable. Under the circumstances, many children are more apt than ever to test the boundaries of their own freedom, and many parents are more likely to exercise control. That vicious circle grows increasingly intense; in the end the child runs.

When minors run they are, of course, breaking the law. (What constitutes a minor in terms of running away depends on the state: it's one who's under sixteen in New York and four other states, under seventeen or eighteen everywhere else.) Runaways may not be lawbreakers in the same sense that youthful burglars or muggers are, but peace officers do have the legal sanction to take such children into custody. Even in states like California, that don't specifically grant this right in relation to runaways, kids can still be picked up under catchall codes. As Section 600 of the California Welfare and Institutions Code conveys, the state's juvenile courts can take over when no effective parental care and control is being exercised over a minor — and minors under eighteen who have left home without permission are presumed to be without such care and control. Even when states specifically exclude "runaway children" from statutes dealing with delinquent children, as Idaho has done, individual counties and cities rush in to fill the gap. They write their own runaway youth ordinances.

The end result is that runaways can be picked up wherever they are, either as delinquents or by euphemistic designations — Persons in Need of Supervision (PINS) or Children in Need of Supervision (CINS). The law is the law, and the law is inflexible. It views all runaway kids as look-alikes: the bored kid who cuts out for thrills, the kid who is afraid to show his folks his awful report card, the kid whose home life is intolerably abusive.

A Delinquent by Any Other Name . . .

Mostly runaway minors fall in the category of "status offenders." That is supposed to take the onus off them. To be a status offender means leaving home, being truant, refusing to obey parental instructions, being incorrigible, using vulgar language in public, having sex, and other such activities.

Of every four girls committed to juvenile institutions each year, three are girls in there on status offenses (mainly because of sexual activities). Of every three boys so committed, one is a status offender. The sexual double standard is alive and well.

A double standard is also at work in terms of class: Most incarcerated status offenders are low-income black and Hispanic youths; most middle-class parents have the money and the know-how to intercede with officials and provide alternatives to incarceration such as therapy, special schools and the like.

It may seem as if status offenders get off easy because the "crimes" they commit aren't serious. But the facts are otherwise. Status offenders are more likely to be detained than youths who have committed serious crimes, and more likely to spend time under lock and key. The younger they are when first locked up, the longer they remain in institutions. Parents who aren't able to cope with their kids can petition juvenile courts to have them declared "incorrigible." There is no similar petition whereby teenagers can have their parents declared incorrigible or incompetent. Even extreme cases of parent-to-child physical abuse are often hard to prove in court.

The status-offender approach to juvenile justice is supposed to be humane, to distinguish status offenses from hard-core delinquency and the commission of serious crime. It aims to provide offenders with psychological, social, educational and medical supportive services. Unfortunately, for the most part things haven't worked out that way. To relabel is not to cure nor to help. Call them PINS, CINS or whatever, these kids are still stigmatized. They're still seen, by the public and, more significantly, by many officials who work with them, as criminals. Should they be housed with adult criminals? Of course not. Yet, despite laws to the contrary, they sometimes are. Should they be housed with juveniles who have committed more serious offenses? No, but — because no separate facilities may be available — they often are.

Even so-called shelters sometimes resemble a Dickensian jail more than they do a rehabilitation center. Kathryn W. Burkhart, author of *Women in Prison,* has told of a children's shelter in New Jersey. The mail is censored. There's no teacher around to teach. The kids get no exercise except in cleaning and scrubbing the place. Solitary confinement awaits kids who commit serious infractions of the rules — infractions like running away from there.

Who protects these juveniles? Certainly not the state legislatures. Many prescribe a host of supportive services for status offenders (Massachusetts is a prime example), then fail to appropriate the necessary funds. There are some practical elements at work, too, pushing status offenders into jail rather than into community-based alternative settings. As John M. Rector, chief counsel for the Senate Juvenile Delinquency Subcommittee, points out, in many states there are financial incentives for housing status offenders in juvenile jails. The state pays up to seventy-five percent of the cost of keeping them in traditional facilities, but only forty to fifty percent if they're in community-based programs.

Under the Juvenile Justice and Delinquency Prevention Act of 1974, the Law Enforcement Assistance Administration (LEAA) is mandated to develop programs to de-institutionalize status offenders. The idea is to remove them from the juvenile justice system. As might be expected, the going is slow. There are a lot of reluctant officials around. Some object on policy grounds — even truants should get what's theirs. Many correctional and police officers and juvenile court judges are reluctant to lose any of their prerogatives. Despite some lofty platitudes on their part, it sometimes seems that what they object to is receiving a smaller slice of the pie.

Kids and Cops

For juvenile runaways all of the foregoing is, in a sense, academic. They simply want to avoid being picked up by the police. They know it may go badly for them if they are. But what does getting picked up actually mean? That depends on the situation and on the policeman in question.

There are many variables. A runaway whose status is discovered because he violates a local curfew ordinance may — should — expect a different treatment than the one caught ripping off a woman's purse. The youth who gives lip to the cop who has stopped him, refusing to identify himself, can expect to receive far rougher treatment than the one who is cooperative. How the individual police officer reacts and what his basic attitude toward teenagers is also play a part. Maybe he despises all adolescents. Maybe he has a special grudge against boys. Maybe he had a bad experience with the last teenager he detained. On the other hand, he may have teenagers himself, may have a good relationship with them and may be favorably disposed toward teens in general.

If the cop dislikes teenagers, he's apt to haul them to the station house just for hitchhiking. If he feels tired and it is almost time to knock off, he's likely to ignore them. If he feels some concern, he may simply talk to a runaway and send him on his way or direct him to the nearest runaway shelter. All this presupposes that the police officer is acting on his own. If he has in hand a warrant to detain a particular runaway, he has no choice but to bring him in.

One thing is certain. The runaway's life-style, especially that of the one who opts for the open road, is fraught with possibilities for police intervention. Thumbing violates the law. So does panhandling. So, in many localities, is being out on the street after ten or eleven at night. So, of course, is dealing in drugs or selling sex.

The climate is different in different areas. In San Francisco, for instance, police officers are generally much more relaxed about runaways than in some small southern cities. In Utah, a way-station to California, cops tend to be hardnosed. In the Bethlehem, Pennsylvania, area some policemen pick up hitchhiking runaways on Highway 22 and bring them to Valley Youth House, a runaway shelter. Many cops in Philadelphia take young hitchhikers to the Travelers Aid Society of Philadelphia. In suburban Kansas City, with its jumble of counties, cities and incorporated towns, cops tend to be tough; more often than not, runaways are detained and tossed into the juvenile justice hopper.

On the whole, though, police officers seem to be more tolerant of runaways than they were a few years back, and to treat them more humanely.

Juvenile courts also vary in how they treat runaways. *The Legal Status of Runaway Children* indicates that in nine states a runaway child "may come within the jurisdiction of the juvenile court as a delinquent child," in fifteen others "as a child in need of supervision." In several other states the language is ambiguous. But juvenile court judges, too, have a good deal of latitude. They can handle the case formally or informally; they can, if they wish, send the runaway home after a pretrial hearing. If there is a suggestion of child abuse they can order an investigation prior to sending the runaway home. But it takes money to provide a service of that kind, and funds for such services are scarce.

"It's Rough Out There"

Today kids who run away to unfamiliar cities find it harder to survive than they did a few years ago. The economic situation makes people less generous. Fear of crime makes people less willing to help strangers, even very young ones (especially young ones, possibly, given the recent spate of publicity about the hard-core crimes and brutalities committed by minors). So panhandling isn't as easy as it once was (though girls do much better at it than boys). Hospitality is far less readily extended; offers to crash come much less frequently.

Roger, sixteen, a big youth in tattered jeans and a plaid shirt, left his native Des Moines and, accompanied by his guitar, struck out for Hollywood. There he hoped to make it big. In what? "In something," he said nebulously when questioned. But a year later all he could show for his grand adventure was a scraggly little reddish mustache. Recounting his experiences, Roger said, "When my brother ran away a few years ago, he had it made. He told me anybody he asked, almost — young people who looked with it, you know? — would put him up for a couple of nights. Not me. It's rough out there. The queers will give you a bed but I don't dig that scene, and the straight guys look at you like you're gonna rip 'em off or something. People are uptight."

Even in generous, tolerant cities like San Francisco, free-food programs have been curtailed or shut down altogether, mission beds have declined in number, public assistance programs have been tightened. And even the grubbiest day jobs are tough for kids to come by, though the more resourceful still manage to find something that will earn them a few dollars.

By now, too, whole neighborhoods that used to be known for their relaxed attitude toward counterculture kids have changed complexion drastically. They have either become more bourgeois or, far more likely, rotted with crime. Tom, a former runaway who now works with new runaways at the SAJA Runaway House in Washington, D.C., contrasts then with now: "Four years ago you could sleep on Dupont Circle at night, just throw down your sleeping bag and crash there. Now — forget it. You'd be lucky if you crawl out of there alive."

Manhattan's East Village, once a crucible for communal

lovingness — forget it, too. Among those cockroach-ridden ruins — or historic tenements, depending on your point of view — only the menacing and the menaced now dwell. Boston — the crash pads there, never great, have degenerated; kids sleep huddled with winos in unoccupied tenements. (Summer is the best time for crashing in Boston — along the lovely Charles River, or in the wooded areas of Cambridge.) Haight-Ashbury, San Francisco's mecca for alternative life-styles, once a fairy-tale kind of place where free food was given out on the streets, has become very nearly burgher-solid middle-class; though some runaways still manage to crash in the area, most hustle on the Tenderloin, competing with derelicts.

Yet even in hard times lots of runaway kids somehow survive away from home. Opportunities are there. American society is big enough, flexible enough to absorb rather than crush the sharper boys and girls. Many become street-wise, road-wise, life-wise very quickly. Barbara learned quickly. Blond and pretty, a sweet-and-sour sixteen, she could look back on three previous runaway episodes. First she ran from the home she shared with her mother and stepfather in a Boston suburb when she was thirteen. She stayed away nearly a week, living with friends. The second time she was away two weeks, with a boyfriend. They slept on the beach in Jacksonville, Florida, smoked joints and had sex under the stars. Barbara returned home feeling better able to cope with the tensions of her life. The third time (that boyfriend long gone) she left for Boston. She wound up sharing a room with ten full-sized kids and a small mutt named Jeff.

Interviewed there, she said, in her wry big-little-girl way, "Call me a three-time winner."

Barbara swore, this third time, that she'd never go back home. She talked, as so many runaway girls do, of step-fatherly affection of the wrong kind. She talked, as so many girls in similar situations do, of a passive mother who was afraid of her man — afraid of his abuse and afraid of losing him.

"She doesn't want to see what's going on right under her nose," Barbara said contemptuously. It was clear that she preferred current hazards to the certainties of the life she had had.

"I spent one cold night here in Boston," she said. "All scrunched up in a tiny alleyway back of the Common. It was my first night. I was practically broke. But the next day I met people — kids who know their way around. They were really nice. Told me the best places to panhandle, where the good corners are, the ones to hang out at when there's a lunch break in the big buildings. They told me about this place I'm crashing in now. I've been here for two months, and it's okay.

"I'm making it. I was a barmaid for ten days. And I'm the one who hates liquor, too, 'cause of my stepfather. It's illegal for a kid my age to sell drinks but in the Combat Zone nobody cares, the cops don't care . . . I met chicks thirteen, fourteen, working the bars. They don't pay you nothin' but the tips are good. I made two hundred dollars a week. But I've quit now 'cause too many guys were grabbing at my tits. Gotta find me another job. Well, I'll make it someplace, somehow."

Meanwhile, even the Combat Zone is closing its more notorious gin mills. Barbara may make it, but the odds are not in her favor.

Survival: Street Scenes and Safe Harbors

Charlie and Sandra

Charlie and Sandra were teenage lovers, runaways together. They were unusually attractive — slim, dark-haired, healthy. They were very young, too — Charlie was only fourteen, Sandra a couple of years older — when they met. And their histories were identical. Both had parents who hated each other and found the demands of childrearing beyond them; both grew up in homes marked by anger and rejection. During one period, Sandra's mother force-fed her until she was seventy-five pounds overweight. Once Charlie, in anguished response to his parents' bitter fights, lost the capacity to walk and had to be temporarily placed in an institution for disturbed children. Both were sent to a boarding school in New England, which is where they met.

They became lovers in storybook manner — intense, all-consuming. Once they found each other their interest in schoolwork dimmed. School officials tried to pry them apart, couldn't, notified their respective parents. Charlie's mother told him, "If you don't stop seeing that girl I'm going to take you out of that school." Sandra's mother threatened the same. The kids knew their mothers meant what they said. They ran away, romantics in a world that places survival in the hands of the pragmatists.

A Greyhound bus took them to St. Albans, Vermont, maple syrup country. They wanted work; they were laughed out of town. Dropping back to Burlington, almost broke, they shared a cheap, foul-smelling flat with a friendly, long-bearded acid freak. He gave them survival tips: how to panhandle, how to rip off food from the local A & P.

Completely moneyless at last, they contacted Charlie's father, who by this time had left his wife and was living in Wisconsin with his girlfriend. He wired them air fare. They stayed with Charlie's father for a bit, but there was friction between Sandra and the father's girlfriend. Too, Charlie's father was understandably uptight about harboring the young runaways, especially since Sandra's suspicious parents were phoning him every few days, demanding to know if their daughter was there. Soon the kids took off again.

They thumbed to Minneapolis, asked around in the long-hair part of town, wound up in an urban commune run on a socialist model. Many of the communards were dropping acid. The commune's leader — call him Ed — found Sandra a job baby-sitting for an alcoholic mother's three children. For twelve-hour-a-day stints she was to get $40 a week, and they were to pay $21 a week for their commune "room," a freezing basement chamber with an old hospital bed in it. Food was extra. So much for Ed's socialist sensitivities.

After a couple of weeks Sandra quit her job. The pair moved to a nearby house owned by the same commune. Then they were asked to lend themselves to a fraudulent scheme whereby the Housing and Redevelopment Administration would give them $4,000 each for moving; they were to keep $1,000 each and give the balance to Ed. They agreed. While waiting for this scheme to hatch, the two runaways were sent to a commune-owned farm; for putting in real working farmers' hours they were paid $21 a week. Ed, ever the exploiter, also wanted Sandra to sleep with him; all the female communards, young runaways or dedicated socialists, were expected to "perform" from time to time. Sandra said, "No way. Charlie's the only one I've done it with." So things rapidly soured and they left the commune.

Incredibly, by now it was a year and a half since they first sneaked out of their New England boarding school with sleeping bags on their backs and some few dollars saved from their allowances in their pockets. Now Sandra was eighteen, no longer a runaway minor. Charlie was sixteen. They decided to find jobs together; it meant creating papers that would make him appear also to be eighteen. What they used was Sandra's birth certificate. First she photocopied it with her name and other revealing information covered over with strips of paper. On the photocopy she filled in the blanks with Charlie's name and other pertinent information applicable to him. Then she photocopied the doctored form. Using the phony birth certificate as proof of age, Charlie got a learner's permit from the motor vehicles department. More proof. Then they got Social Security numbers and found jobs in the same place, a company that liked young people who were willing to put in long hours for little money. When last seen, there they were, selling something over the phone and only marginally starving.

Choices to Make

Runaway teenagers may not have more than the clothes on their backs and a little change in their pockets, yet one thing they usually do have in abundance is choices. Their choices all pertain to survival. As a result of the ones they make, they can wind up smarter. They can become more appreciative or more contemptuous of the homes they ran from. They can end up more bitter, more cynical. They can, increasingly, become "lost children." Their choices can make them age ten years in ten days; it can make them into addicts or dropouts for life; can make them into hustlers supreme or put them in touch with their altruistic feelings.

In sum, the choices they make while away — all the more so if they're away for a considerable length of time — can significantly and sometimes irrevocably affect their futures. Rarely does a boy or girl who is away from home for more than a week or two, and spends a lot of time on the road, escape unchanged.

But how do kids make their survival choices? A number of factors are involved. Their savvy. Their natures. The degree to which they're emotionally stable. The extent to which they're self-destructively angry with their parents — the extent to which they feel compelled to want to say, "See all the rotten things I've had to go through because of you! Aren't you sorry?"

Sex and Survival

Much has been written about the exploitation, principally the sexual exploitation, of young runaways. There has been publicity aplenty about the way tender-skinned young adolescent girls are sucked into the world of prostitution or become stars in pornographic films and magazines. The media concentrate on this and to some girls of course it happens.

It happens. Go to the teeming Port Authority Bus Station in New York City — or to any big-city bus station. Watch the buses, one after the other and on weekends especially, disgorge the teenagers. Here they come, like chickens down the conveyor belt ready to be plucked. And there to do the grading and the plucking — canny eyes casting for the most attractive of the young girls, the gentlest of the young boys — are the rail-thin, smart-stepping, broad-brim-hatted pimps. The Port Authority has its own youth squad, but it is too big a place, with too many gates and too much movement, to allow for more than cursory protection.

So the pimps, mostly black and very smart, scramble for the "packages," as suburban kids about to become whores are called. Master psychologists, they play on a naive girl's vulnerabilities and on racial guilt.

If a girl succumbs to the pimp's sweet jive he buys her a meal, then clothes, then puts her up or gets her a room, has sex with her, makes her feel like a queen in the wormy part of the Big Apple. In a few days, though, reality crashes down upon her like a migraine. She has to earn the bread. If she hesitates or tells him no he gets some of the girls already in his stable to persuade her what a fine and easy life it is, how much money they make, how much the pimp likes her and how special he thinks she is. She's scared of the stone jungle, she's down to her last dime — what the hell, why not give it a try? Her father's been hassling her about only being interested in boys and sex anyway; might as well *be* a whore — but just for a little while — as be falsely accused of being one.

That's one scenario; there are other, even uglier ones. Back to the Port Authority Bus Terminal. See the buses disgorge the little girl splitters atremble with the thrill and the fear of it all. See them standing lost and helpless, easy for the cunning dudes looking for young prey. See two girls, once young but a little older now, a worn seventeen or eighteen, settle on their victim. She's blond, round-faced, a bit plumpish — a cherub of a kid. They approach, introduce themselves, offer to help. The girls seem so nice, so warm and friendly, that the cherub is awfully flattered and feels reassured. Eagerly, she follows them, and winds up in some sleazy pad, drugged, then pumped full of smack to boil the innocence out of her. Then she is gang-raped. Then more smack, more of the same. Then she's out on the street, an instant addict, hustling the rough customers on Eighth Avenue, the dregs.

For a while a lazy white pimp in the East Village simply sat in his pad, negotiating his trade. Unsuspecting runaways, both girls and boys, came to him. Why? Because he ran ads in the *Village Voice* offering runaways a place to crash. When they arrived he farmed them out to his clients, gays of both sexes and all ages.

Recently a Port Authority pimp picked up a fourteen-year-old from Long Island, took her to a fleabag hotel in midtown Manhattan, kept her at knifepoint and repeatedly raped her for three days; then he took her outside the Hilton Hotel to turn tricks for him. For once, the scheme backfired. She ran inside instead and got help; the pimp was arrested.

Two girls ran from home, a small town in Pennsylvania, and started hitchhiking to New York City. Young guys full of laughs picked them up and drove them to the Queens headquarters of a scabby motorcycle gang. They were gang-raped by nearly forty youths, taken to another house, gang-raped again, and kept prisoners for several days until they managed to escape.

Not all the teenage girls who become teenage prostitutes are so victimized. Some already know, even before they board the bus for the big city, that that's how they'll make their way. Some are recruited in other states, then sent to the eastern markets. Pimps in Minneapolis have a lucrative slave trade going for them; they recruit young runaways from well-to-do Minnesota suburbs and rural areas. So many girls are sent to Manhattan that Eighth Avenue has become known as "Minnesota Strip." In 1975 New York City police found fifteen teenage prostitutes all recruited from the same small town in Kansas.

However they get to prostitution as a way of "making it," the street soon chews up these girls and boys who go on a constant regimen of sex and drugs. Vacant-eyed and hollow-faced, they become caricatures of their former adolescent selves. Yet many — most — don't ever want to go back home. They feel they've sunk too low. Or they're still consumed with hatred for what they left.

The Runaway Squad

Sergeant Jim Greenlay is a big, bluff, concerned man with teenagers of his own. He's with the New York City Police Department's Runaway Squad. It is his job, and his partner's, to cruise the city's likeliest areas, ferret out teenage runaway-hookers and arrange to have them sent back home. New York — that cold, uncaring city — happens to be the only city in the country with such a special squad. When runaways make serious allegations against their parents, an effort is made to contact juvenile authorities in their home areas, but the children are still sent home. There's no money available to do anything else with them. And while the kids keep coming to town in sizable numbers, like matrons rushing to a Bloomingdale sale, the Runaway Squad has gone through the city's fiscal washings and shrunk markedly.

But on this day Sergeant Greenlay feels good. The night before, he saw a sixteen-year-old girl reunited with her father. She'd run from her middle-western home in the wake of a broken love affair. It was her second such failure; the first time she threatened suicide. Her parents refused to see how emotional she really was; they disregarded her dramatics and she, feeling abandoned, ran away. Like so many other kids, she wound up in New York City. Her transformation from small-town girl to big-city whore took a week. Luckily, her new life came to an abrupt end because she called her father from an Eighth Avenue bar. He managed to have the call traced, then contacted the New York City police. They asked him to fly to Manhattan; accompanied by Sergeant Greenlay, he went to the bar and found his daughter there. Father and daughter cried; father and daughter embraced; father and daughter went back home. Happy ending — there are precious few of them on Eighth Avenue.

The Runaway Squad prowls mainly where teenage hookers offer their wares — Times Square, Twenty-ninth and Madison, the Bowery, and, of, course. Eighth Avenue from Forty-second to Fiftieth streets, a jumble of seedy bars, porno shops, dirty movie houses, clairvoyants and souvlaki joints. The squad concentrates on girl runaways, Sergeant Greenlay explains, because of limited manpower. "Boys can assimilate into a crowd more readily, they can get jobs faster — it's easier to pick up the girls."

Maybe other factors also play a part. Boy runaways also often become prostitutes — and gays, boys or men, are not your policeman's favorite charity.

Homosexual Runaways

But the Runaway Squad doesn't forget about boys entirely. Sometimes it scouts for them at the homosexual locations in Manhattan — Fifty-third Street and Third Avenue, Central Park West on the park side of the street, the squalid subway stations and penny arcades of Times Square.

"Chickens," as the boy hookers are called, are frequently recruited at bus stations just like the girls. Sometimes they go willingly. Other times they are also beaten and drugged into submission. But many runaway boys, homosexually inclined, know how to make their own contacts. Underground and gay newspapers tell them just where the action is in New York City and in other metropolitan areas. These papers also run "looking for a roommate" ads. The boy who answers hopes for a kind, understanding middle-aged lover; he may be brutalized instead and thrown out on the streets to play boy hooker. Los Angeles police estimate that around 30,000 children, mostly boys from six to seventeen, are sexually exploited in the Los Angeles area.

The hot line at the Gay Community Services Center, in Hollywood, California, gets plenty of calls from teenage boys, many of them incipient runaways. These are anguished boys, tortured sons. They want to — but can't — tell their parents of their homosexual leanings. They feel — they know — what the reaction will be. But they don't want to live the straight life anymore. So, in time, some boys in this predicament see their solution as running away from home. They reject, before they themselves are rejected. Others, who do experience parental rejection after coming out of the closet, run at that point. Some are teenagers. Many are young adults — eighteen, nineteen, twenty or a little older. And when they run, lots of them still head for southern California — the land of hope, the repository for impossible dreams.

"A lot of people I see in this office really believe that when they come to California the streets will be paved with gold. There's going to be happiness and the possibility of a part in a movie," observed a young counselor at the Gay Community Services. "It's true even more of the young kids than of the rest. It's amazing, the disparity between what's going on inside their heads and what they're actually doing. They'll go out and hustle. They'll go in drag to try to get somebody to pick them up so's they can get a place to stay for a couple of nights. Instead of being resourceful young lads they project an image of helplessness. They exploit that, it's the way to get by.

"Yes, people respond to that and abuse them, but they still get food and a bed. They drift from place to place, situation to situation, and inside their heads they're just wanting to be discovered for a movie, or to end up in Beverly Hills, or

to become a surfer. They tell awful stories about what some
old lecher has done to them — tied them up in bed, behaved
sadistically — and still they expect the kind of openness and
access to the top rungs of the ladder that's not possible for
a kid without money or connections. They're exploited wherever they turn — by the unprincipled lechers, by the American dream; finally, they exploit themselves."

Crash Pads, Communes — and Being Had

So exploitation is a fact of life, a condition of existence,
whether the runaway be gay or straight, young adult or cal-
low youth. Not that exploitation goes on all the time with
everyone, not that every teenager is exploited or exploits
others, not that there aren't good times, rich moments,
beautiful experiences. But whatever choices the runaway
makes, from hitchhiking to crashing, the potential for exploitation — and for danger — is there.

Many girls hitch rides without incident whatsoever. A
few, like the pair from Pennsylvania mentioned earlier, get
trapped into something brutal. A few panic in response to
an overly friendly male driver; they jump from moving
vehicles, bruising themselves or breaking bones. Some,
cozying up to their drivers, stay with them for a few days,
maybe sleeping with them, maybe not, cooking and cleaning
in exchange for a place to crash. Girls tend to think of
young men as safer to ride with. Some observers of the
thumbing scene, though, say that older men are actually less
apt to take a hitchhiking teenager on an unwanted sex
trip — that these men tend to be kinder and less inclined
to risk trouble. Common sense suggests that neither course
is without great risk.

As for crashing, the whole business of shelter clearly
carries with it the potential for exploitation. Crashing may
mean a mission bed, a cheap hotel bed provided by a con-

cerned Travelers Aid station; it may mean staying with friends or friendly adults; it may mean rooming for a few days with a friendly college student (it is not unusual for college students to give temporary shelter to young runaways, on campus or off); it may mean informal crash pads or communes, or religious communes or runaway houses.

Crash pads and communes, those eloquent expressions of youthful solidarity so popular in the late sixties, have been on the wane. Says Cheryl Steinbuch, a social worker at Manhattan's The Door, "The sixties are over, the days of the crash pads are gone. It used to be you could come to New York City and somehow, by grapevine, by underground, you could find a commune to crash in for two weeks until you felt like moving on or until you got a job. But these places are becoming fewer and fewer. The communes that we knew about have shut down. If they continue to exist it's like a very closed shop. There are just less freedom and more restrictions. People are not trusting people as much as they did in the sixties."

So much for urban communes. As for the rural ones, also so popular in the sixties, most of the middle-class kids who were in the vanguard of the back-to-the-earth movement simply dropped out, as should have been expected. Boys and girls raised on a steady diet of television, stereo, handsome allowances and a bountiful supply of junk foods aren't going to enjoy the working farmer's life-style for very long, no matter how much they may despise their parents' money. In some places, however, communes still flourish — in upstate New York, for example, and around the Topanga Canyon and Laguna Canyon areas of Los Angeles. In the latter places communards live in a handful of tents and shacks, growing natural foods, making jewelry and crafty things out of hemp, which they sell from roadside stands.

Where exploitation occurs, it's most often in the area of sex and drugs. In some crash pads and communes it's understood that girls will show their appreciation by means of sex, boys by dealing in drugs, both by panhandling. It may not seem like exploitation when a sexually experienced seventeen-year-old girl is asked to sleep with other communards, and it isn't if she is free to make the choice. But if sex is a condition for receiving shelter, and she has nowhere else to go at the moment, it's another story. If immature and hungry runaways are pressured into selling dope, they're choosing to deal, of course, but it is also exploitation on the part of those who profit by their endeavors.

None of this is to suggest that all crash pads and communes try to exploit those who use them as way-stations. It all depends on the place. For several years now a very ethical commune has flourished in downtown Los Angeles, near the University of Southern California. There anybody over eighteen can crash for a week or two, no questions asked. People who want to stay on for longer periods are expected to show commitment to the communal way of life — either by taking on outside jobs and contributing their earnings to the commune, or by working in the commune itself, sorting nuts and bolts for light manufacture in the area.

There are other communes like that one. On balance, however, it's probably safe to assume that more crash pads and communes are potentially exploitative settings than not.

Religious Communes
And not to be overlooked in this context are the religious communes. As old as humankind's earliest religious communities in one sense, they are also the new order of the day. Run by sects like The Children of God, Agape, Hare Krishna and the Unification Church, these communes attract young and disillusioned adults who seek instant spiritual regeneration in the cults' authoritarian structures. Most are in their late teens and early twenties, but in some cases younger

teenagers, runaway teenagers, have also been finding their way in.

Many of them come from highly permissive homes, and structure is what they desperately want; many are on drugs and want to get unhooked. The rigid cult life — most cults ban drugs, alcohol and nonmarital sex — gives them exactly what they want. At least for a time. Eventually many young people find the cults' inflexible approach to life, their lack of tolerance, too confining.

Cultist leaders steadfastly deny harboring juvenile runaways; they have yet to convince suspicious parents, who believe the worst. In the hard-coal region of northeastern Pennsylvania, for instance, twenty-eight families, all with missing children, accused a fanatical evangelical sect, the Forever Family, of harboring them. Counselors at Berkeley Youth Alternatives, a licensed runaway house in Berkeley, California, have taken in several teenagers who were painfully disillusioned with their lives, had hopes for spiritual regeneration, then became more disillusioned. They ran from home, ended up in a religious commune, fled when it failed to give them the spiritual nourishment they'd sought.

A family counselor in the Los Angeles area counsels a few teenage runaways who, far from being eternal and eternally empty-handed wanderers, lead remarkably well-ordered existences. Their sanctuary is a religious communal movement like Agape — but they go to school and show up regularly for their therapy sessions.

The Good Samaritans

A matron in a suburb of Minneapolis has acquired a reputation among kids who split from home; when runaways show up at her door, tipped off by others who have already enjoyed her hospitality, she offers them shelter. A New York high school teacher who lives with his wife and children in Manhattan's Chelsea section gives temporary asylum, from time to time, to teenage runaway friends of his children, and occasionally to others he happens to encounter.

Such people exist, here and there, throughout the country. Sometimes they shelter runaways with the full knowledge and approval of the parents involved — in which case the teenager's status changes from "runaway" to "living with another family." Sometimes they allow kids to live with them secretly, even though it is against the law in every state to harbor runaway children without their parents' consent. Their rationale: "These kids need help, and no one else is willing to help them." And, "They're better off with me than in a dangerous situation or in a police station." They see themselves as performing acts of kindness and decency. And so they are, in their fashion. Often they have a strong empathy with adolescents — and a bias against parents. Some have had abusive mothers and fathers themselves. Some have felt like failures with their own children. Motivations vary; altruism doesn't exist in unalloyed form.

Some youth workers are critical of the Good Samaritans, especially the ones who fail to work with parents. One worker said, "These people are being exploitative, too. Not in terms of sex and drugs necessarily, but in other ways. They welcome runaways to stay with them, then weave a seductive spell — 'what terrible parents you have, stay here as long as you want.' It's a rebellious, mindless kind of parenting born out of these people's need to be rebellious. Runaways need a respite from home, they need safe environments, but they also need new insights and perspectives into their circumstances."

Says Sister Marlene of the Minneapolis runaway house, The Bridge for Runaway Youth, "I don't trust people who feel sorry for somebody. Because then they usually do something that is not going to help that person grow."

The Runaway Houses

In the mid-1960s there was none. In 1976 there were at least 130 of them, most properly licensed, in forty-two states.

The first runaway house in the nation, Huckleberry House in San Francisco, was started in 1968, in response to all the runaway kids, many of them broke and needing medical attention, who were overrunning the area. Then others began to spring up in San Diego, Washington, D.C., and other counterculture meccas.

In the beginning the houses had a precarious existence. Funding was very hard to come by. The establishment — including police and the entrenched social service agencies — was hostile to them. The early runaway youth workers, most of them very young, many former runaways themselves, earned that hostility. They were almost as rebellious as the youths they served. Many hated the establishment, including parents. They became single-minded child advocates — failed to enforce rules, plotted against parents, fought with the cops, railed against the establishment agencies and tried to keep themselves and their shelters together with driblets of money. They were accused of being poorly trained, allowing chaotic conditions to prevail, and sometimes working against the best interests of the youths they sheltered. It was all true, but it was also true that counterculture runaways for the most part spurned established mental health agencies, because of their rigidities, their bureaucratic approach, and the medical model of pathology with which they approached their young clients. Understandably enough, the attitude of counterculture and otherwise rebellious youths was — and is: "I don't want to go to anyone who sees me as crazy."

A number of shelters failed. The ones that didn't have, for the most part, grown. New ones have sprung up. Funding, while still difficult, is not the problem it once was. Money for shelters and shelter programs has come from various sources, including the National Institute of Mental Health, the Law Enforcement Assistance Administration, state and city youth departments, charities and church groups. Moreover, in 1971 Senator Birch Bayh introduced the Runaway Youth Act to provide low-ceiling grants for shelters and services; it became law in 1974.

All this interest, this activity and this generosity were inevitable. Children have always run from home, but once hordes of middle-class kids began to do so and their parents clamored for help, it began to be seen as a significant social problem. Hearings on juvenile delinquency conducted by Senator Bayh helped focus attention on the runaway kids. A sensational murder case in Houston, in which twenty-seven boys (wrongly identified as runaways) were slain, also helped things along.

With expansion and with funding more readily available from the bureaucracy, the runaway shelters themselves have inevitably become more professional and more bureaucratized. They scrabble for funds, they fight among themselves at conferences. But their staffs are better trained. Usually they include at least one or two certified social workers, trainees from local schools of social work, youth workers and a heavy complement of volunteers — teachers, feminists, musicians, carpenters — sensitive, perceptive men and women, it is hoped, who like adolescents well enough to work for relatively low pay or for nothing.

Now, on the whole, police and community relations are far better than they were. Now in-house rules — among them no drugs, no sex, no violence, no weapons, curfew hours and an obligation to do chores ("You're worse than home," some runaways say disgustedly) — are enforced. Regulations requiring parents to be notified of the runaway's presence within twenty-four to seventy-two hours of his arrival, depending on state law and the policy of the particular runaway house, are usually followed.

Runaway houses offer their young guests free room and

board, and a chance to sort out and begin to confront their problems. Stays range from a few days to a few weeks, depending on the house. Generally, shelters can make legal, medical and employment referrals when necessary. They provide a variety of psychological services, which are always necessary but not always welcomed by the runaways. Most houses offer psychological counseling — individual, group, family. (Family counseling can work only when parents live nearby and are willing to participate; often they're not.) Most have "linkages" to psychiatric services. Some run group homes; most can arrange for foster care if the youth's home environment is so destructive as to make a return home unwise. Some have grown to the point where they have outreach programs, working with school and community groups. Boston's The Bridge has its famous, fully equipped medical van, which parks nightly in Harvard Square to bring medical services to runaways, street people and other youths who'd never think of going to a regular doctor's office.

Even the process of living with other kids in this kind of alternative setting with its own rules and expectations can be helpful sometimes in giving young runaways a different perspective about themselves and their problems. As Carol Tweedy of Seabury Barn in suburban Long Island says, "Almost without exception the kids come into the program with the idea, 'My life would be beautiful, I would be a beautiful person, if I could just get rid of my parents who are messing up life for me — it's all their fault.' Well, they come here and they can maintain that fantasy for about two days. Some who are really good at it can carry it for as long as a week. That's the honeymoon period. Then they start to experience problems in living here. And then they're going to have to take a different look at themselves."

As might be expected, things are still far from perfect insofar as the operation of the runaway houses is concerned. Some young staff members persist in seeing parents as the "enemy." Occasionally a youth worker especially sympathetic to a particular runaway will hide him and not notify his parents. Staff turnover is a big problem. Many counselors and administrators find themselves "burned out" after working intensively with troubled young people for a few years. Foster-care placements aren't always made with the greatest attention. Money is still often tight and leadership not as good as it should be.

How good are runaway houses? Bill Treanor, who helped draft the Runaway Youth Act bill and is Project Coordinator for National Youth Alternatives Project, which provides technical assistance to runaway houses, says, "A third of the programs are exemplary, a third so-so, another third could stand quite a lot of improvement."

For all their inadequacies, runaway houses are a constructive, rational approach to what really is a social problem of considerable concern.

Making It Somehow

Regardless of how thick youth workers' beards are, or how long their hair, runaway houses to some extent are becoming part of the establishment. Many runaway kids avoid them, and for a variety of reasons. They want to make it on their own, think shelters are "sissy." They don't want their parents notified. They don't like the rules. They like the idea of living by their wits and of outwitting the law.

In fact, the ability of runaways to survive as runaways often depends on how much they can get away with. When teenagers have little chance of getting jobs, medical attention or shelter (in many places runaway houses aren't set up, or are full), then manipulation and illegality become inevitable. There are people around who will help them. Sympathizers, persons out to profit from their predicament, or both.

Free clinics and hot lines aren't supposed to refer minors to informal crash pads; some do. Some keep lists of private individuals who have "extra rooms" to accommodate runaways but don't necessarily check them out carefully. Travelers Aid officials in San Francisco and elsewhere have seen some young runaways who complained of having been asked to go on sex trips in such circumstances. That free bed doesn't always turn out to be so free. The clinics or hot lines that refer minors when it is against the law to do so make a pro forma effort to see the runaways' credentials "proving" they're over eighteen — or a letter, written by the runaways' parents, giving them permission to travel by themselves.

Of course, a letter that looks genuine needn't be, and identification that looks bona fide can be phony. Whether or not the document is genuine isn't important to such clinics; they simply want to protect themselves legally. The clinic or hot line may even send the runaway to a place that makes up fake IDs. In San Francisco, for example, there are a couple of shops — one on Market Street, the other on Golden Gate Avenue — that for a few bucks and a passport photo will transform a fifteen-year-old into an eighteen-year-old. Too, as Sandra and Charlie demonstrated, a lot can be done with a genuine birth certificate and a photocopy machine.

An enterprising little publishing firm in California is struggling to maintain the counterculture philosophy. Advertising in the underground press, it offers official-looking but wholly meaningless "state ID" cards for $5. Why anybody would accept such cards as genuine proof of anything is a puzzler, but apparently people do. Still, the publisher must be aware of the fact that its product needs some shoring up. One of its fliers advertised free with every ID order an official-looking numbered blank birth certificate, with "certified copy" stamped in red. It suggested filling out the form appropriately, making a photocopy, then using that copy as the "official" birth certificate.

Some hardened runaways are impatient with the idea of writing letters or filling out forms. They adopt a more aggressive means of obtaining identification. They snatch purses or wallets for driver's licenses and other such useful items.

Jobs are anathema to some runaways imbued with the counterculture ethos that rejects all capitalistic ways of life, but many other runaways are glad to find something that will earn them a few dollars. They scour neighborhood merchants, shopkeepers and cafes. Somebody might turn out to be looking for cheap labor that doesn't have to be put on the payroll. With nearly two million illegal aliens in the New York metropolitan area alone, most of them working, really persevering American runaways, especially if they look older than they are, can find something. Runaways have found work waiting on tables, washing dishes, cleaning up in markets, working as barmaids. When jobs are scarce, however, more and more girls turn to prostitution, which may also seem more attractive than menial kinds of labor.

In college towns some sophisticated runaways take advantage of the system. They hang out on campus, rap with friendly students, learn how students get outside jobs through the school, head for the college work center and fill out the proper form — putting down their real names and false but genuine-seeming student identification numbers.

Clearly, the older and more sophisticated a runaway looks and acts, the more easily he can take advantage of such survival techniques. The more willing he is to take any job on a temporary basis, no matter how dirty it is, the longer he's able to maintain himself on the road. Older runaways who have learned some marketable skill in high school — typing, for instance — have an advantage. Looking and being older, possessing fake identification papers, they can easily pass themselves off as eighteen or nineteen, thus standing a better chance of snaring office or factory jobs that pay a lot more than does shoveling a market's garbage. Soon they're lost in the crowd, soon they're really eighteen — and then, suddenly, they're legal. It happens all the time.

Trapped on the Street

Older or younger, the runaway youths who fail to return home can also go to the other extreme and blend in with the street crowd, the street people. Even if they remain for months on end in a particular neighborhood, the grubby street people's neighborhood, becoming fixtures there, street people are psychologically always on the run. By no means are all recent runaways. On the contrary, some have been homeless practically from birth. Some others are "throwaways." But many did split sometime back. As The Bridge's Sister Barbara Whalen puts it, "They're runaways of the past who are still nowhere."

They lead sad and poignant lives for the most part, these sixteen-, seventeen-, eighteen-, twenty-, twenty-two-, twenty-five-year-olds. They "hang out" much as high school kids do, but for them hanging out isn't a passing phase. They live in hallways, they live twenty to a room. They have little food. They sometimes make do with mission handouts or, if things get too bad, scrounge around the waste that markets throw out.

Their eyes are hollow, their skin pasty, they don't look *well*. They've just taken in too many drugs, too much booze. They've been undernourished for too long. Some are persistent panhandlers. Some get in on the fringes of criminal activity — stealing, dealing, pimping, prostitution. As Stephen Torkelson of Covenant House, a Manhattan-based shelter, points out, "If you live on the street for more than one to three months you've got to be abused, and you've got to abuse people."

Many street people congregate in places like Berkeley and Cambridge and Ann Arbor — university towns — maybe to be close to the lost dream of their own education, their own whole lives, certainly to cash in on the more liberal climate and abundance of free services available in those towns.

Dr. James R. Oraker, staff psychologist at Dale House, a runaway house run by the Young Life mission to teenagers, paints a gloomy picture of the outcome of the street life. "The longer a youth is on the street, the more wasted he becomes," Dr. Oraker says. "The longer he's on the street, and using drugs, the more pronounced his symptoms become." They're frightening symptoms that suggest these youths have already crossed some indefinable boundary of functioning, that they will never again be like the rest of us. There is loose association, fragmented thinking. In the language of the street, they become spacey. Some are schizophrenic. Their youth ebbs quickly: to be twenty and to look forty is one of the badges by which the street person is identified.

Yet many of them, like most teenage runaways, come from homes familiar to us. Our homes: homes of business people and professionals, of white- and blue-collar workers, homes the more class-conscious among us are fond of calling "respectable." So what brought them to the insane life of the streets? What prompts teenage runaways in general to make a break with their histories, to walk out on their families? In many homes, too many homes, troubled parents are asking themselves these troubling questions.

5

Cause and Consequence: Why Kids Bolt

Revealing Interviews

"How long have you been away from home, Josie?"

"Two weeks."

"Guess you stopped off someplace before coming here."

"I was gonna come straight to Boston but this dude in a Karmann Ghia — I flip out over Karmann Ghias — gave me a lift. Well, he did a whole number on me, like I was the greatest looking chick he'd ever seen, and he just wanted to take me home and introduce me to his mother."

"That must have been nice to hear."

"Well, I know I'm good-looking, but he did have a real nice way about him, and I sort of went along with it. So we got to his place, an old farmhouse or something, way out in the country. It was okay but I felt kind of spooky at first, there was nothing there — nobody around."

Josie laughed and toyed with a strand of her sunny blond hair. "Guess you know what's coming. His mother wasn't there and he pretended to find a note from her, like she'd gone to visit her sick sister in the next county. Then he wanted to take my picture and we went out to where there was a creek and took pictures, and . . . "

She shrugged her thin shoulders; her voice trailed off. She was asked, "He put you up for a while?"

"Yeah, till now. I mean, like he was nice, but he expected me to do everything for him, do the cooking and cleaning up, and take care of his dogs and cats when he went to work. I didn't mind that, because he did put me up and he was kinda sweet, even if he was old, like thirty-five."

"Did he lay a sex trip on you?"

"That was weird, like he didn't touch me or anything, the whole time we were together. All he wanted to do was to take pictures of me without any clothes on, and then he'd go off and play with himself."

"Was there any particular reason you left?"

"Sure. Yesterday morning he got out a whole drawerful of socks, said they needed darning. That's when I split. Darning somebody's socks is definitely not my idea of fun. So I walked to the highway, took me nearly an hour 'cause he wouldn't drive me, and thumbed to Boston. And here I am."

"Have you gotten in touch with your folks at all since you've been away?"

Josie's large, expressive gray eyes narrowed, suddenly hard. "What would I want to do that for?" she demanded suspiciously. When no answer was forthcoming she offered a hostile shrug. "They don't give a shit about me anyway."

"Is that why you left home — because they don't give a shit?"

"I left 'cause they were hassling me to death. 'Be in by eleven, not a minute later. Don't go out with Carl, he's not nice. Josie, why don't you clean your room, it looks like the

pigs slept in it. Josie, what's that I smell on your breath?'
They were treating me like a baby and I couldn't stand it any
more. I told 'em I was gonna run away if they didn't stop
treating me like a baby, and that's just what I did."

There she was, Josie from Connecticut, fifteen years old and
a runaway in Boston, having come to town with a temporary
stop somewhere in rural Connecticut. Now, newly arrived at
a runaway house, she was undergoing "intake" — an initial
interview — with a sympathetic counselor.

Josie is all too typical of runaway teenagers, especially the
younger ones and the first-timers. They tend to trivialize
their reasons for running. They like to zero in, huffing with
outrage, on those stiff parental rules and regulations that
keep them feeling "like a baby." Or, when asked why they
ran away from home, they say they don't know, they aren't
sure, they know they were unhappy at home but it's all fuzzy,
out of focus, they can't give their unhappiness clear shape
and form. *You were unhappy, that's why you ran? Yeah,
that's it. Unhappy about what? I don't know, man, just
wasn't good, I just had to leave, had to get outa there . . .*

If the questioner keeps pressing, their replies become vague
and mumbly. They don't have the patience for this kind of
self-scrutiny. They become evasive. There's nothing shrewd
or calculated about it, though. It's an evasiveness, often, over
which they have no control. Some come from homes in
which they and the other family members have had destructive relationships for a long time. But nobody ever acknowledged it. Nobody ever talked about it. Nobody ever talked
about . . . *dangerous things* . . . so how could these young
people suddenly be expected to acquire the skill?

Yet, during one of the counseling sessions that follows, if
there is a chance for them and if the counselor is good
enough, some opening up occurs. So it was with Josie. Here's
what emerged: her parents were constantly, hatefully fighting.
What about? The father's other women, the way the kids
were being brought up, the way the kids behaved. More: they

blamed each other for Josie's wildness, for her older brother's drug problem. If Josie's mother cracked down, her father thought she was being too harsh; if her father cracked the whip, her mother turned protective. Both drink; recently their imbibing has taken an ominous turn: they've grown loud and bitter; they've slapped each other and have also threatened to hit their two children.

So it went as Josie talked — an ever darker, chillier depiction of her home life. And the bravado with which she kept saying, "I don't give a shit," and "I don't give a shit about them," gave lie to the words. She did care. She was anguished. After all, she felt tormented enough to run.

This is true of the majority of them, the vast majority of these girls and boys who bolt out of their houses or sneak away in the middle of the day or night vowing never to return. They're caught up in a paradoxical situation: when they run they choose to go, it's a conscious decision, yet they feel compelled to make that particular choice. The feeling of being trapped compels them. The feeling of being wounded — and wounded and wounded — compels them. The anger, the fury, the wish for revenge, the unconscious hope that these people *will* give a shit after all, compels them.

No More Huck Finns

Where, then, are the Huck Finns of old — at least the mythical Huck Finns — the eleven- or twelve-year-olds who save up the dimes from their paper routes, hop on a bus, and go off to the big city? Such youngsters do exist. They often run in pairs, bold, bored kids in search of a little excitement; they often end up at some Travelers Aid booth — broke, scared, thrilled too, but ready to go home.

"They represent such a small, small part of our caseload of juvenile runaways," said Catherine C. Hiatt, on the verge of retiring as head of the busy Travelers Aid Society of Washington, D.C. "We call their mothers and they say, 'Thank goodness, send them home.' Even three or four years ago there were more of them than now; now we get fewer adventurers than ever before."

What the folks at Travelers Aid now mostly see among their young clientele, what the runaway houses mostly get in the way of temporary guests, what turn up most often on seedy city streets and warm Florida beaches and in offbeat counter-culture areas are kids like Josie. Kids who feel intensely pressured. Maltreated. Unwanted. Behind walls of studied indifference or defenses based on inarticulateness are unfortunate family dramas like hers. Dramas in which no role is that of winner or hero. All the characters suffer, all can rightly claim to be maltreated by life's circumstances.

Abusive Parents

It has often been noted of child abusers that they were themselves abused as children — sufferers trying to make up for their own suffering by inflicting it on others. Though most studies and reports of abusive parents focus on young children, teenagers too are victims of parental brutality. Parents who beat up their teenagers are found both in the Harlems and the Scarsdales of the land. Fourteen-year-old Tommy, who lived in Harlem, swears his father beat him with a tire iron whenever he got drunk. And he has the scars to prove it. Tommy eventually ran away. Bea, whose home is in upper-middle-class Pacific Palisades, in sunny southern California, says her divorced mother slapped her around whenever she got on a sherry-drinking jag. Bea eventually ran, too. Not a small minority of runaways leave because they've been victims of a pattern of physical abuse. The Center for Studies of Child and Family Mental Health of NIMH estimates that adolescents comprise fifteen to twenty percent of all physically abused children.

In recent years the problem seems to have been increasing. Economics very likely plays a significant part. A violence-prone parent who is made panicky by money problems and an abrasive and rebellious teenager make an unhealthy mix.

It has often been observed in the case of severely abused little children — those with burn marks on their backs or fractured limbs or cuts on their bodies — that they don't want to leave their abusive parents. They don't want to be yanked from home and placed in more protective environments. This is especially so if the abusive parent is the mother; the maltreated child is apt to cling to her as if she'd just been voted Mother of the Year. Mother love, separation anxiety, a fear of the unknown, all probably play a part.

What has this to do with abused adolescents? Some of them have the same clinging feelings about home. They may have run from home when they think they've had enough or when things get too bad — but the tie still does bind. If they don't acknowledge it directly, their behavior does.

Take Sheila, who came to Seabury Barn, the runaway house in Long Island, exhibiting severe bites inflicted by her mother. Yet, within a few days, she became so homesick she wanted to go back home — and did. Some other abused adolescents like her force the issue indirectly; they violate runaway house rules to such an extent they're asked to leave. At that point their thinking is, "Well, since I've got nowhere else to go, I might as well go back home."

Says Seabury Barn's director, Carol Tweedy, "Kids and parents can be screaming, fighting, even beating each other up, but there's an interaction. Interaction — that's where the value is for them. They don't know how to — or can't — elicit a positive response from their parents but they know how to elicit a negative response. And that's better than nothing."

Incest, More or Less

Next to sibling incest, father-daughter incest is the most common kind (incest in general is far more prevalent than popularly believed). And, indeed, some teenage girls do leave home because their fathers have become, or were on the verge of becoming, inappropriately affectionate.

Many more split because of their stepfathers. The pattern is banal, if unpleasant. A girl's divorced mother remarries. Things are fairly quiet until the girl becomes a curvy adolescent. The man of the house contrasts his middle-aged wife with her nubile daughter, and there's little doubt as to which of the two arouses his sexual fantasies. Quite possibly there's some flirtatiousness on the girl's part, too, since she's at an age where she has the need to compete with her mother. The stepfather's fantasies acquire increasing urgency; finally — often helped along by drink — he persuades her to engage in some form of sexual activity. Then again, she may be a willing partner in a seduction scene. This may not be incest in the strictest sense of the term, since the stepfather isn't related to her by blood, but few would argue that the event classifies as sexual abuse. Even if she has helped the seduction along, the girl involved frequently finds the guilt feelings that are generated more than she can bear. She can't face her mother. So she runs away.

Stepfather or father, seduction need not be carried to its ultimate conclusion to prompt a girl into running. A study of runaway girls conducted at the Framingham, Massachusetts, Court Clinic and published by the *American Journal of Orthopsychiatry* describes what may well be a widespread family pattern. Forty-two girls were involved. Their ages ranged from thirteen to seventeen. While only three of the girls actually accused their fathers of incest, the psychiatrists who studied them saw a consistently destructive family pattern at work among them all.

In each case the parents' relationship was poor both emotionally and sexually. The parents lacked control over their impulses, especially their sexual and aggressive impulses. The fathers drank heavily at times and went into violent temper tantrums. Many engaged in extramarital affairs. On the surface, the mothers appeared to be the stronger, more dominant personalities in their families. It was a sham. Underneath, they were depressed, felt themselves to have been rejected by their own mothers, and viewed themselves as inadequate in their roles as wives and mothers. Both parents found it hard to control their daughters' behavior, too. The girls lacked control in the same areas their parents did.

Without realizing what they were doing, the mothers responded to their feelings of inadequacy as wives by shifting the burden to their daughters. In effect, this kind of mother would tell her teenage girl, "You do for him what I'm not able to." As the study's authors put it, "In addition to rejecting her husband sexually, the mother also encourages a warm, close, eroticized father-daughter relationship from which all three derive considerable satisfaction."

For a time that causes no serious problems. But as the girl matures physically, things begin to change. Words from the study again: "With few effective controls demonstrated by either parent, the fear of overt incest comes uncomfortably close to consciousness, and the intimate relationship between the father and the daughter now becomes threatening to both."

Now all of the participants in this sad little psychosexual drama go into their respective, inevitable acts. Dad becomes angry and restrictive toward his daughter. He accuses her of sleeping around — often a projection of his own wish to sleep with her. As might be expected, daughter rebels. The form her rebellion takes is to become seductive with boys and men outside the home, perhaps actually to have sex with them. And where's mother in all of this? She is in the middle. She wants to keep on encouraging daughter to do what she does. She also wants to protect her from the realistic dangers involved. The tension builds and finally gets to be too much for daughter. She runs.

Children of Divorce

Clearly, these ways of relating can occur whether the male parent involved is the natural father or the stepfather. But children of divorce are susceptible to runaway episodes for reasons other than those relating to incestuous longings.

One major reason has to do with the *assumption of adult responsibilities*. The teenager lives with a single parent and a number of younger siblings. Constantly harried, depressed, lonely and beset with money problems, this left-behind parent can't cope with all the demands of her brood as well. She begins to feel that since the teenager is the oldest child, he or she should take the place of the missing parent insofar as the other children are concerned. So the teenager becomes a quasi-parent, though still needing his own share of parental warmth and attention. What he gets instead is short shrift, and not even enough time to be with his friends. Sooner or later he says to himself, "There has got to be more to life than this" — and runs.

In some single-family settings where the brood is large and the pattern of delegated parental responsibility ingrained, each child-parent runs away at sixteen or so, never to return. It's attrition at a steady rate until the family is practically destroyed.

A second major reason children who live with divorced parents run away is *to be with the parent who doesn't have custody.* This is how it was with fourteen-year-old Tim, a tousle-haired runaway from Tennessee. who He lived with his mother. They began to fight nastily almost as soon as he reached puberty and began the normal process of adolescent assertion. Tim thought more and more about his father. He hadn't seen him in three years, hadn't heard from him in a year and a half. But he remembered his father as a great guy. Tim was convinced that his father, now living in Florida, would understand him in a way his mother did not. So he ran away to find him.

It was in Washington, D.C., while munching on a hamburger in a greasy spoon near Dupont Circle, that Tim told his story to a sympathetic journalist. He was going to find his dad, he was going to live with him and everything would be okay. Did his father know? "No."

Did he know where his father lived?

"Well, in Florida."

But Florida's a big state. Where in Florida?

"In Jacksonville, maybe. Yeah, somewhere around Jacksonville."

Hope you make it okay.

Tim looked up from his plate; enthusiastically he said, "If I can just get down there I'll find him. He'll straighten everything out."

They Run from "Nice" Families, Too

It is no problem at all to collect horror stories of runaway kids who were so brutalized physically or emotionally as to make one wonder why they didn't run sooner. But what about runaways who come from other kinds of families? Intact families? "Decent" families? "Nice, respectable" families? Why do the kids suddenly run from homes that seem to be having only their normal quotient of arguments and conflicts until a runaway episode jars them out of their complacency?

To hear the runaway tell it, the reason for running was relatively trivial. "I ran because they hassled me about keeping my room clean."

"Because they kept after me to do something about my hair — my clothes."

"Because they said I was on the phone too much."

"Because they didn't like my boyfriend."

"Because they kept bugging me to do better in school."

Whether or not the parents involved hear reasons such as these to account for their children's leaving, they're often

genuinely baffled. *But things weren't that bad,* they sometimes insist. Yet if things hadn't been that bad their children
wouldn't be running. The counterculture runaways of the
1960s may have had their own serious problems but they
also had a "carrot" — places to run *to,* the youth festivals, the
crash pads, the hordes of like-minded kids they knew they
would encounter all along the hippie trail. There's no carrot
out there today to make running more attractive. It is a
rough world, and many kids know it. When they run it's because they feel they have to.

Thomas H. Waner of the Family Service of Los Angeles, a
social worker who works with many runaway youths in the
San Fernando Valley area of Los Angeles, says, "Their anxiety level, brought on by the tensions at home, is so great that
they have to get away — have to give that level a chance to
get down."

Adolescent Rebellion

Adolescence is a legitimately confused time. In one way or
another, all adolescents rebel. They must, as part of the devel-
opmental process of learning to separate from their parents
and become independent members of society. Many adolescents, early adolescents in particular, see themselves as possessing a maturity they don't really have. This prompts them to
make a radical demand: "Don't treat me like a kid anymore;
don't set any limits on my behavior."

That demand notwithstanding, the idea of assuming adult
responsibilities makes them want to scurry to the safety of
their homes and pull the covers over their heads.

They resent their fear, their continued need for protection — resent these feelings so much they redouble their
rebelliousness. "I won't let you tell me how to live my life!"
is a refrain common to most young rebels.

To greater or lesser degree all youths are subject to these

push-pull pressures of dependence and independence. To "prove" their independence some adolescents go to extremes. Adolescents who run from "nice" families are sometimes in this position.

Question: Why do runaways need to go to extremes? Why can't they deal with those push-pull conflicts the way other kids do?

Answer: Because in their lives there's more going on than those surface conflicts about clothes or hair or curfew time or boyfriends or the use of the phone or chores would indicate. Beneath lies a plethora of hurt feelings, of accumulated grudges, of unmet needs and expectations, of disappointment piled one atop the other. Both the teenager and the parents have been subject to these dissonant elements. There may also be near-insurmountable temperamental differences; sometimes parents and their children can't seem to get along no matter how hard they all try. In either event, for some adolescents deep-seated family problems produce reactions far graver and more painful than normal teenage rebelliousness.

Scapegoats and Noncommunicators

Family interaction is no simple process of cause and effect. Rather, it's a junglelike growth of action and reaction so tangled the wonder is that family members don't trip up more often than they actually do. Again, this holds true for every family, the "nice" one as well as the one where gross pathology is evident. Whatever kinds of families runaways come from, the counselors who work with them must untangle the interactional undergrowth to find out what's really going on.

One thing that often goes on is marital friction, tension, conflict. Husbands and wives don't need to shout bitterly or throw things at each other for the conflict to be a palpable aspect of the family drama. All too often, in order to fool themselves into believing everything is fine between them, couples pretend theirs really is a healthy partnership when it is not. Mutual warmth, affection and concern may have been replaced by a never-ending undercurrent of hostility, but parents prefer not to admit it. Facing up to it would, after all, mean having to do something about the situation. This is something they're not prepared to do. So the two partners are in collusion. Their goal: to pretend everything is okay.

Yet hostility felt is hostility expressed, and mothers and fathers such as these often express it covertly (and unconsciously) through their children. The expression can take many forms. Here are a few:

One parent makes "gentle" fun of the other, directing the remark to the child and inviting the child to join in.

One parent undermines the other's authority.

Mother and father disagree intensely on disciplinary approaches — one's too lax, the other too tough; they can never get together, work together. This leaves the child feeling confused, angry and guilty. "They're always quarreling about me, so it must be my fault."

Both parents pick on the child. By making him the focus of their dissatisfactions they can avoid coming to grips with their hostile feelings towards each other.

Thomas Waner of the Family Service of Los Angeles flatly says, "The child who runs is the family scapegoat. By singling out that child, by making him the scapegoat, the rest of the family can maintain a kind of equilibrium."

Poor communication is another causative pattern in the families of runaways. "Poor communication" has become a cliché, so often is it used to explain marital and parent-child relationship problems. Still, if feelings, wishes and attitudes can't be expressed, miscommunication and misunderstandings are inevitable. If people can't express their needs, these needs remain unmet, making resentments and hurts inevitable.

Teenagers are especially prone to disguise their real feelings. Sherry is an example. She is fifteen. Whenever she's out with her boyfriend, becomes sexually overstimulated and feels pressured by him because he wants to have sex with her, Sherry returns home sullen and angry. She becomes rude to her mother and father.

This is a fairly typical situation, and her parents have two choices. They can focus on her bitchiness. This will generate a lot of hostile words but Sherry's ambivalence — the problem that's making her act this way — won't get dealt with. On the other hand, Sherry's parents can be good listeners. They can try to "hear" that their daughter's sullen behavior is a cover-up for something of genuine concern to her. They can, gently, try to unearth what it is. Even if Sherry isn't willing to tell them right then and there, they can open the way for frank, supportive discussions later.

The parents of runaway children generally don't know how — or don't bother to try — to get at the thoughts and feelings behind their teenagers' acts and words. Communication in such homes is, or becomes, a sometime thing, at least about issues more sensitive than the weather. The kids involved may be civil to their parents but keep mum about most of the things they think, feel and do that are really important to them. They live together, such parents and children, as distrustful strangers. The atmosphere is one of quiet alienation.

Childrearing by Extremes

Also prominent in the "normal" families of runaways are parents who go to extremes in raising their children — either being much too restrictive or acting at the outermost limits of permissiveness.

At a family service agency in Massachusetts, caseworkers talked about a set of nice parents who dedicated themselves religiously to family togetherness. For instance, every Sunday afternoon, no matter how old or uninterested they were, all the kids had to accompany them for a drive and dinner out. Finally their seventeen-year-old daughter, reacting to their many demands in the name of togetherness, ran away. Her folks were such nice, loving people; she couldn't bear to hurt them. More accurately, she couldn't rebel openly — couldn't face them directly to reveal her really urgent need to be her own person rather than their satellite.

Caseworkers at the Family Service of Los Angeles in its San Fernando Valley branch tell of another nice family. This is a large one of six children. The father is a kind-hearted, strong man, a benevolent dictator. Among other things he has worked out all the children's day-to-day schedules of activities, including precisely when each child is to use the family bathroom. Two of his teenagers have already run away. A third is on the verge. The father cannot understand why.

These true-life examples may seem overly dramatic, but they illustrate the point. Rigidity is anathema to most teenagers. They have one unfailing measure of what's fair and unfair, and that is how things are handled in their friends' homes. Betty may put up a ferocious squawk if Susie down the block is allowed to come home a half-hour later than she is on weekdays. But a half-hour isn't that big a deal, the situation is tolerable. If Betty is expected to come home an hour or two before most kids in her area, however, it makes her family's standards so different from mainstream norms that she herself is made to feel different. Then the situation becomes intolerable.

Parental rigidity can have many causes. "That's the way my parents did it with me," is a commonly expressed one. It's as though such mothers and fathers are saying, "My parents treated me as if they owned me and, by God, that's the way I'll treat you."

Another common cause, a basic reason for inflexibility on parents' part, is insecurity. Such parents think, "If I'm not tough and strong my kid is going to take over." Extrapolating,

"Either my daughter's going to be completely chaste and pure or she'll become promiscuous. Either my son doesn't touch a speck of pot or he'll become a pothead — or worse."

"Sometimes they even have huge fights around what color the kids' bathroom should be," Carol Tweedy says. "They're big power fights. It's hard for many of these parents to back off and allow for different kinds of attitudes, behaviors and life-styles. They see their kids in terms of ownership and control. Basically it all boils down to, 'Who's in charge?'"

When parents and children are engaged in a power struggle, no amount of compromising has any lasting effect. The parents say the kid can go out two weekday evenings, the kid says four. They compromise on three. Soon the kid yells, "I'm being treated like a baby!" Really at issue isn't two nights or three or four, but the whole pattern of relations between these parents and the adolescent.

Parents and children often fight about schoolwork. The Metropolitan Washington Council of Governments' report on runaway youths in the Washington area puts academic pressure at the top of its list of reasons why boys and girls say they run away. The same thing probably goes on in all upward-striving, competitive communities and neighborhoods. Because parents have traditionally tended to place more pressure on boys to perform well in school so they can get good jobs, it's boys more often than girls who give "hassles over grades" as a reason for having run.

Whether they're boys or girls, youths who run because they're not performing to their parents' high standards feel, "My parents don't love me for myself but for what I achieve." Or they feel, "I'm not worth anything except as I achieve." When they run it is ostensibly to escape the relentless pressure or, if their marks are poor, to elude the wrath of hurt and disappointed parents. What they're really running from, though, is a life at home where they consider themselves unloved, worthless children.

If many runaways hail from rigid, pressuring homes, many

others come from families where pressure is a dirty word — and permissiveness is exalted. Consider Doris. Doris was allowed to urinate on the carpet as a child and to come and go as she pleased when she became a teenager. Doris of the milky skin and sculptured face was last seen hustling out-of-towners in the New York Hilton. She comes from money; she's third-generation Scarsdale.

"They were so hung up on money and position they didn't give a shit about anything to do with us except put us in fashionable schools and dress us up in expensive clothes," Doris said, referring to her parents. "My two brothers and I had all the spending money we needed. They never noticed that their sons became speed freaks and that I was screwing like mad. One day my father's main business associate tried to get into my crotch. I let him. Later on I told my father about it, just to see what he'd say. He said — get this — 'Well, Doris, you're a sophisticated young lady now, you can take such things in stride.' He and this man had a big business deal going and he didn't want anything to fuck up the works . . . "

Nothing so dramatic in Paul's life. Paul, a stocky youth with a nice grin, was last seen in a runaway house in Colorado. He comes from Cleveland and his family is comfortably middle-class. His father sells stocks. His mother is involved in volunteer work. Paul and his two older sisters were pretty much left to themselves.

Describing his growing-up years, Paul said, "Nobody ever raised a voice in our house. I don't think I can even remember Mom and Dad quarreling once — or hassling us. They liked everything low-key." He doesn't remember them kissing, either, and said they weren't demonstrative with their children. House rules were minimal. He and his sister could eat whenever they wanted, and as he got older the whole family rarely dined together except for Thanksgiving, Christmas and when it was some family member's birthday. Home, as Paul pictured it, was a place in which everybody touched base but nobody really touched each other.

What finally drives teenagers like Paul and Doris to run isn't an excess of parental dos and don'ts but an absence of them. Adolescents may set up a guerrilla cry for "freedom," but when they're truly freed in the sense of being allowed to do as they please they become as edgy as if they had no choices at all available to them. Dr. Oraker of Dale House sees many runaway youths who come from extremely permissive homes. They're apathetic. So, it would seem, are the other members of their families. The people involved don't reach out to each other. They don't holler. They don't argue. There's no passion.

"Home," Dr. Oraker says, "has become a kind of a place where nobody cares about anybody, so why not see where the action is?"

He draws the difference between rigid and overly permissive parents: with the rigid ones everything is conditional — "I'll love you *if* you do this and this"; with the permissive ones "nobody goes out of their way to show love, there's no affection." The end result in both instances is a kid who doesn't feel loved.

Something else of great importance goes on with many boys and girls who are reared in highly permissive households, households where few or no limits on their behavior are set. They may pretend to like being "free," running wild if they have a mind to; actually, they experience life as if careening in a brakeless car, experience the terror of being out of control and expecting to crash in some horrible way.

When they run, permissively raised boys and girls don't generally do so because of some catastrophic event in their lives or because of extreme tension at home. In fact, they don't so much run away as drift away. "Since their families don't care, what's the point in staying, is how they feel," Dr. Oraker says. "They drift because there's nothing at home to really hold them."

On the road they like to be left alone. They're inoffensive — bland, gentle, apathetic, quiet. They're superficial in their ways — committed to nothing but desperately hungry for the love they'll never admit they need. It is hard to reach them and help them, because they don't consciously want to be reached, don't consciously want to be helped.

What Is a Runaway?

We love to label: it's easier to deal with definitions than with people. During the Depression, runaways were classified as juvenile delinquents. For years the American Psychiatric Association's reference work on mental illness, *Diagnostic and Statistical Manual of Mental Disorders,* has been listing the "runaway reaction" as a major childhood disorder. Incredibly, this "scientific" conclusion was drawn on the basis of a study of three hundred runaways in the New York State Training School for Boys.

A more realistic study of nearly one thousand runaways in Prince Georges County, Maryland, an affluent Washington, D.C., suburb, concluded that there are two groups of runaways — a seriously disturbed minority and numerous other children "troubled in much the same way that other adolescents are troubled." This NIMH-sponsored report, known as the Shellow Report, concluded, "The problems facing most runaway adolescents are the same as those facing many other young people; in this sense, running away from home can be seen as one way of dealing with these problems. Other adolescents deal with these problems differently, but not necessarily in ways better for themselves or for the community."

It is certainly realistic to conclude that running away is no more destructive, in and of itself, than boozing it up on weekends, committing vandalism, withdrawing or dropping out, or getting hooked on thrill pills.

Following the establishment of the runaway shelter network, a task force of runaway-house counselors and administrators worked out a profile of the "typical" runaway. This is what task force members came up with:

The runaway is impulsive. (Impulsiveness is a predominant characteristic of adolescents generally, but runaways have it to a greater degree — they're easily distracted, more readily given to impulse stealing, more capricious in situations requiring them to make decisions.)

The runaway can't delay gratifications; frustrations are intolerable. The runaway's motto might be, "Never later — *now*."

Socially the runaway's temper runs to extremes — to loneliness and withdrawal or to a desperate clinging to peer groups.

The runaway doesn't trust adults. He — and she — have a hard time making their anxieties known. Their way of life is to "act out" rather than "talk out." They have a low sense of self-esteem; given most of their backgrounds, that's hardly surprising. They think "magically." If they press the right button, they believe, everything will be okay.

An example of magically thinking teenagers: unhappy girls who think that happiness will come to them if they get pregnant, marry the fathers of their unborn children and move away from home. They do get pregnant. But then their script goes awry, for either their boyfriends won't marry them or their parents won't let them marry. Often, in such cases, they run.

What Teenagers Need

In order to flower during their adolescent years, teenagers need clear rules that they've had a hand in establishing. They need structure — intelligible structure that makes sense in the context of their lives. They need a sense of trust — the feeling that their parents trust them, that they trust their parents. They need rules and structure applied with a reasonable degree of consistency. They need to feel respected. They need self-respect.

In sum, what teenagers need, runaway teenagers usually

don't get. It's the responsibility of parents to accord their children the same positive rights of self-determination and self-respect they seek in their own lives. Simple to propose, endlessly difficult to achieve. Too often parents seek in their sons and daughters what is missing in their own lives and take more than they give; or, just as bad, demand too little of themselves and of their children.

PART THREE:

The Adults

6

Vanishing Husbands: Unnerved, Unmanned, Undone

Bert's Odyssey

Now here's Bert — not a teenager escaping from his parents, not a rebellious adolescent but a thirty-six-year-old man, muscular, good-looking in the old John Garfield tradition. Bert, a tough but bright and articulate product of one of Ohio's industrial areas, an adult runaway, a runaway come home.

Let's color his background in swiftly. They're colors of youth, fear, naiveté. Bert eighteen, Mary fifteen and pregnant — two scared kids sneaking through back alleys one night to reach the local Catholic Church. Happy day, happy night, they were getting married — skulking through the town's least trafficked streets in the dead of night because that's the way their families and the priest wanted it.

The marriage, begun in such a fragile way, lasted a full

twelve years and caused five children to come into the world. But, according to Bert's account, the only warmth it generated was when he and Mary had sex. In bed, and only in bed, were they well suited. Otherwise there was no sharing — no sharing of concerns or feelings.

"I wasn't the hearts-and-flowers kind of guy," Bert says. "But I think I was a good husband and good father. I allowed Mary to go out a couple of nights a week. I thought she was with girlfriends."

In blue-collar towns men do not take it lightly when they're cuckolded. Yet when Bert discovered that his wife was sleeping with another man he decided, mostly because of the kids, to stay with her. In turn, she swore she'd stop seeing her lover. She didn't. She started drinking heavily. Briefly, she saw a psychiatrist. Bert became what he calls "half-separated." Part of the time he lived at home. The remainder he spent at a friend's house.

Laid off from the factory he worked in, he collected unemployment checks and turned the entire amount over to his wife. (He himself lived on the earnings he made working on the sly for a building contractor.) But then his wife's drinking and sexual adventures became more blatant. One day he couldn't stand it any more. He beat her up.

"In this town you don't talk about your feelings, you join the football team," he explains wryly.

After battering his wife, however, Bert felt guilty. For a time he stayed away from her. Then she hurt him in a way more cruel to him than her infidelity had been; she sold the nice old house that was half his but in her name and moved herself and the children into a housing project.

"It blew my mind," Bert says. "She sold our house. It was a killing offense."

He knew his rage, knew he was capable of killing her now, knew he had to get away. He'd been thinking of leaving, playing with the idea. That's all he and two of his buddies, all married, had talked about over beers for the past several weeks — splitting, leaving, running off somewhere, escaping. They longed for "freedom." They dreamed of the distance they would put between themselves and their nagging wives and, in the case of those who had children, their demanding kids. The brews they downed made it easy for them to see their delightful destiny: manly adventures and pretty women.

So when Bert felt that his only options were either to kill or to run, he told his buddies it was time to stop playing and start packing. They packed.

"The three of us abandoned a total of three wives and seven children," Bert remembers. "If it wasn't for me they wouldn't have gone. Seems like I was getting thrown out of one tribe and starting another."

They finally left, one weekend afternoon, with a few hundred dollars between them. They took one car and headed for the Gulf Coast. Boozing and whoring was their immediate project. Their bacchanal lasted two weeks, when everybody except Bert had gotten the poison out of their systems. Each, unbeknownst to the others, made a forgive-me-honey phone call home. Sheepishly they said good-bye to Bert and headed back.

Bert telephoned his wife, too. She said, "I want you back." He said, "No."

But he also talked to his children, then to his mother and sister, and from then on made periodic phone calls to them all.

Phone calls didn't assuage the rage Bert felt. This was an angry man, a man who felt cheated by life. He worked — mostly in construction — but drank a lot. And fought. He looked for imaginary slights as an excuse to punch someone. Once he got into a fight with all of the men drinking at a rough bar. Another time a motorcycle gang he'd provoked burst into his motel room and beat him up. Once, after a fight, he wound up in jail. Later he was to read several popular psychology books on emotional awareness and become more sensitive to his actions.

"I thought I might be killed in those days," he comments reflectively now. "I think subconsciously at the time I was looking for someone to finish me off."

No one did. He quit construction, left the area, got a job tending bar in New Jersey, then went on to Virginia, where he managed a magazine-selling crew. He made himself quit drinking so much. He turned to marijuana, smoking grass heavily because it mellowed him and made him less combative.

Nearly a year had passed since Bert and his buddies staged their mass runaway. He still called Mary sometimes, but because he never could get enough money together to send some back home, she went on relief. Local authorities tried to locate him; they also pressured Mary to start divorce proceedings. He became involved in an auto accident. He was unhurt, but because of the reports that were filed, Ohio officials located him. That prompted him to quit his job and move to Florida.

Florida, living this time with a call girl, Glitter-bug Sally. When he first met Sally in a Miami bar she wasn't a call girl yet, just a pretty and lonely girl in her mid-twenties whose marriage had broken up. She'd been sleeping around a lot. Shortly after she and Bert began their affair, they decided to live together. He signed up with a magazine crew again and got her a job selling. She was an excellent saleswoman, mainly because she was willing to barter $50 worth of subscriptions for a half-hour's worth of sex.

Half-jokingly (or so Bert later claimed), he told her, "If you're going to give your ass for magazines, why don't you sell it outright?"

Sally replied, "I was going to talk to you about that."

So she went to work for a man who owned a local business, and who used her to butter up prospective buyers. She made $500 a week and gave most of it to Bert. He was her lover, companion, protector.

"From the point of view of hedonism, those were the two happiest years of my life," Bert was to say in retrospect.

"All I had to do was hang around and be happy — drinking good whiskey, watching the Miami Dolphins. I learned to love her. Learned to love what she was doing for me. I went from a nine-to-five foreman in a factory to being a small-time pimp, you might say."

His good feelings about the life he was leading lasted for about a year. Then he began to feel more and more uncomfortable. He'd see kids and miss his own. He felt guilty about his neglect of them. He became harshly critical of himself and of his life. He pitied himself, too. These signs let him know that his runaway period was up. It was time to go home. He told Sally, who wasted no time finding herself another protector, then went back to his home town in Ohio. A divorced man now, Bert got a job in a foundry. He met a nice young woman. Their relationship has flowered. He seems devoted to her, and is again living the life of a rooted man.

Of his three-year hiatus as a runaway husband, Bert's assessment is mixed. He reckons, "I've learned to become more liberal, a lot more open, more sensitive to myself and other people." But his children were "acting funny" toward him; they didn't know what their mother had done to precipitate his running and thought he simply abandoned them. In many ways he was having to start from scratch, he says, and while his runaway time added to his life "they were also a lot of wasted years."

Midnight Calls and Other Patterns

In some respects Bert is hardly the prototype of the runaway husband. How many men slip away from their families in the company of two other runaway husbands? How many live with call girls? How many stay away as long as he did?

Yet in other respects Bert's story does coincide pretty closely with those of married men in general who run away from home. Like him, they think for a time of running. Some kind of crisis occurs. Dreams of escape become a real-life act; they make the break.

As was the case with Bert, that break most often isn't absolute. They make calls home. They return home, most of them, as Bert's friends did — within two, three, four weeks. By then they've had enough of the fugitive life; they want to get back to the world they're familiar with.

The telephone calls that runaway husbands make are sometimes referred to as "midnight calls." And with good reason. They do often occur late at night when the children presumably are asleep. The runaways don't want to disturb their children, and don't want to be disturbed by hearing their voices. Unlike Bert, many runaway husbands don't complete their initial calls. They want to make the connection, want to hear their wives' voices, but don't want to talk. It is too painful — or embarrassing — to have to say something. So they call and listen. The conversation, if it can be called that, is difficult. Hello? *Silence.* Jim, is that you? *Silence.* I know it's you, Jim, please say something. *Silence.* Please, just let me know you're all right. *Click.*

"I just wanted to hear her voice sometimes, and know she was okay," one midnight caller explained. In his narcissism he forgot how hard it was on his wife; all he knew was that he needed that tenuous link with home. It reassured him somehow: even if his own world was in turmoil, there was stability at home; the voice he was so accustomed to hearing was still there at the other end of the line. It was as much contact as, at the moment, he could manage. One deserted wife, counseled at the Family Service of Dedham, has gotten two calls from her husband in fifteen years. He ran fifteen years ago.

Why They Run

What are the circumstances that drive family men to disappear from their families? In the long run, an accumulation of angers, resentments, disappointments, unmet expectations in relation to their wives and possibly their children, as well.

In the short run there are usually precipitating events. A financial crisis is one of the most common. One typical pattern: a man goes wild on those little plastic credit cards, feels himself drowning in a sea of debts, doesn't know how to keep afloat, panics, runs. Another pattern: a man doesn't get a raise, promotion or bonus he's been promised and on which he has been counting heavily, both to get himself out of debt and to restore his sagging sense of self-esteem. He sees himself a failure, he sees those around him seeing him a failure; it's more than he can bear and he runs. A third: a man loses his job, can't get another, is convinced he has let himself and his family down. As the days and weeks and months go by without a job he feels himself falling apart. At last he can no longer stand it; he runs.

In the early 1970s, when massive layoffs hit the aerospace industry in southern California, there ensued a striking number of desertions among engineers' families. For both the husbands and the wives those engineering jobs had represented the ultimate in stability and had helped keep some of the families together. When unemployment struck it was like an earthquake toppling a jerry-built structure; those families, those marriages, fell apart. Some spouses separated legally, some ran away.

But not all men who run for economic reasons do so to escape the specter of failure that has been shadowing them. There are those who run away to better their status, something that seems to be especially true of working-class runaway husbands. As a Los Angeles detective who has been involved in a number of such cases laconically remarked, "A guy making six dollars an hour digging ditches says to himself, 'Hell, I can go someplace else and do better.' Or maybe he just wants a change."

Just wants a change? It is really not that simple. A husband and father who can leave his family as easily as he can go on a weekend fishing trip can hardly count marital and parental satisfaction among his blessings. "Unhappy home life" is clearly an element in most if not all runaway husband cases. Even if a failure to get a raise or high indebtedness or loss of job is the major stress, the tensions that result are apt to have a corrosive effect on the marriage.

Of course, there are men who flatly say, when asked why they've run, "It's because of my wife." And what is it about their wives that impels them to be so dramatically rejecting? Giving their obviously one-sided reports, these runaways point to wives who keep pushing and pushing. "No matter what promotion I get, no matter how much money I earn," they say, "it isn't enough." They point to wives who have taken on lovers. They point to wives who nag and complain, bored wives, wives who want more attention, more love (unreasonably so, as far as these runaway men are concerned). They point to wives who have changed in some significant respects. Time and again, caseworkers are told, "She's not the woman I married."

Could the women's movement have something to do with such changes? According to F. Stowe Hull, executive director of the Travelers Aid Society of Philadelphia, it has. His caseworkers, he says, see an increasing number of husbands who run away because their wives have become active in, or influenced by, aspects of Women's Liberation.

Stowe outlined the kinds of men who respond most unfavorably in these cases, and the family configurations they're apt to have run from. The husband hasn't been an active participant in family life to any appreciable extent. He works all day, comes home, drinks beer, watches television, is a weekend father. While he's the ostensible "boss" in the family, his wife actually runs the roost. Things go along like this for a long time. But then she joins a consciousness-raising group or is otherwise affected by the women's movement. Her stifled dissatisfactions come to the surface. She's no longer willing to play the game. To make up for the feelings of deprivation that now run so strongly inside her, she becomes assertive, demanding. Her husband is stunned by the transformation. He's in no shape to judge the legitimacy of her new demands. Suddenly he's in no shape for anything. He skips.

Changes strike hardest and most painfully those marital unions that are symbiotic. Symbiosis characterizes relationships, marital and otherwise, in which the two people have a relationship so close as to defy separation. Their "love" for each other is so powerful, so ardent and all-consuming, that they see their world as created and populated only by themselves. They depend on each other mightily and are greedily possessive. Each sees the other as an extension of self.

Stanton Peele, a young professor at the Harvard Business School, proposes that such people are not so much in love as caught in the grip of an "interpersonal addiction." Addicted or not, they use each other to fulfill all of their psychic needs. And they leave each other when those needs are, for some reason, no longer being fulfilled. At times, leaving takes the form of desertion, especially if one of the partners still wants to hang on and the other has found a replacement.

So it was with Joanna and Harvey, two thirtyish Chicagoans locked into a symbiotic marital union that change unbalanced and desertion ended. "We were like two peas in a pod," Joanna said afterward, an incredibly wistful look on her small, thin face. Outside observers might have concluded that Joanna lived solely to please Harvey, and that he could do pretty much as he pleased. Very likely, though, that was the way she wanted things, too. Now and then Harvey disappeared for a night without explanation. Joanna didn't ask where he was, and if such things made her resentful she kept the feeling hidden even from herself. As she told everyone, she considered herself lucky that such a man, such a vital and successful businessman, loved her.

What created the imbalance in this perfectly balanced union was Joanna's accidentally becoming pregnant. She wanted the baby but told Harvey that if he was unhappy about it she would get an abortion. He told her not to. But she later learned that he told friends, "Now that we're going to have a baby, my life is over." Then, three months before the baby was born, he disappeared, leaving her bereft and his business partners in the lurch.

Other men, other pressures, other dreams, other reasons for desertion. There are men who run away with other women, there are men who run away with other men. It is far from uncommon for a man in his middle years to discover that he feels more comfortable and rewarded sexually in homosexual alliances. Or, to have had such alliances sporadically throughout his life and finally decide to commit himself to a homosexual way of life. If he runs away it is because he can't face his wife, his children, his parents, his friends, his work companions.

Much publicity has been given the mid-life crisis — in which a man in middle years realizes he's getting old, takes stock of his life, and finds it wanting. Whether such a crisis is inevitable is the subject of endless debate. But certainly such crises are common, and in the most virulent forms produce depression, impotence, a sexual hunger for younger women, alcoholism, lots of anger and restlessness, dissatisfactions with everything and everyone, as well as separation and divorce. In some men it also triggers desertion. These husbands claim they're not so much running from as to something — to a new life on an organic farm in Vermont, to artisanship in hippie shacks, to wild and heady romances with girls barely older than Lolita, to attempts at acting or painting or writing. They need to try, they need to take a break, but few tailor the dream to the size of possibility. Few make the dream come true. Most at last give up and return home, hoping for forgiveness and forgetfulness. And a few end up, having lost everything, as suicides, mental patients, or bench-warmers on skid row.

The Poor Man's Divorce

Let's not leave out alimony and child support. In good times and bad there are men whose running away is primarily motivated by the idea that if they run they won't have to pay for their freedom on the installment plan. What is commonly known as the "poor man's divorce" evokes a stereotype: the boozy, irresponsible black man who leaves his wife and gigantic brood to wend their lonely way to the welfare office after he's long gone. The fact is that black men, white men, Hispanic men, men who are poor, those who are very well-off, those who fit all economic gradations in between are represented among those who take off because they don't want to pay.

According to an official of the Office of Child Support Enforcement, federal estimates have it that close to 3.3 million "absent parents" are associated with welfare families. Many are deserters, others are ex-spouses or separated spouses who have skipped out on payment of child support. While there are few socioeconomic data to support specific conclusions, the impression of those involved in child support investigations is that it is increasingly a middle-class problem.

The Massachusetts Child Support Enforcement Unit, for instance, numbers teachers, doctors, lawyers and businessmen among such runaways. Chuck Schultz, who heads the Parent Locator Service in Minnesota, estimates that about twenty-five percent of the absentee parents his unit tries to find are middle- and upper-middle-class, earning in excess of $15,000 yearly. Most of these are young professionals and executives. One man who sticks in Schultz's mind — and craw — is a veterinarian who earns considerable money but won't pay the child support he owes his ex-wife for their several small children. Because of his profession he can find employment wherever he goes — and does he go! Whenever Schultz's office tracks him down somewhere he slips away for parts unknown.

Middle-class, yes. But it goes without saying that the middle-class family whose principal breadwinner absents himself today is likely to become the welfare family of tomorrow.

To the extent that the "poor man's divorce" really is the poor man's, some powerful rationalizations for it can be presented. There is the obvious fact that he is least able to pay. The poorer and less educated he is, the more suspicious he is of law and lawyers (though many a more sophisticated person has come to adopt the same attitude). As for Legal Aid attorneys: despite the fact that many low-income people still don't know free legal services are available to them, Legal Aid offices often have long waiting lists. What's more, legal separation and divorce are time-consuming; desertion accomplishes the same thing with the speed of a slammed door.

Cynics will say that many desertions among low-income groups are phony — merely stratagems for getting the family eligible for relief payments. A popular image has the supposedly absent breadwinner sneaking out the back door every time the welfare worker comes snooping around. According to a 1975 study of welfare families in New York City, that picture is about twenty percent correct. The study found about one of every five welfare mothers has separated from her husband or lover or live-in man in order to get on welfare.

Ill-framed welfare laws, not only in New York City but all over the country, practically solicit such chicanery. They flatly discriminate against the intact family in favor of the female-headed one. In 1975 a family consisting of husband, wife and two children, living in New York City, didn't qualify for welfare if the husband earned $5,500 or more. On the other hand, if he played the game and pretended to desert, he could still keep his job, earn his $5,500 — while his wife would get about $4,000 in cash from welfare plus other benefits like food stamps and Medicaid.

Ironically, phony desertions frequently turn out to become the real thing. Say a low-level worker and his wife collude to have him "desert." He moves out but, following their prearranged plan, continues to see his wife and children. Then he gets caught up in his new life as a single male. He finds other women, unencumbered women — women more attractive than his wife. So he sees his family less and less. Eventually he disappears altogether.

All of the foregoing presupposes that a fairly stable relationship preceded the man's departure. But few stable relationships can exist in slum settings shot through with drugs, alcohol, violence, gambling, the highest unemployment rates in the city and rotten schools. Moreover, numerous ghetto families tend to be from the rural south and "multipopulous" — that is, consisting of mother, lots of female relatives, loads of children and men — fathers and substitute fathers — whose status in the household is often transitory. They're victims of social and economic forces beyond their reckoning and out of their control — forces that encourage welfare and desertion as a way of life.

Bittersweet Revenge

By and large, runaway husbands aren't great planners. It can't be said of most of them that they meticulously chart the paths they will take when they flee hearth and home. At the same time very few literally slam out of their houses with only their clothes on their backs. There are all kinds of approaches to running away; what happens depends partly on the man's nature and partly on how responsible he feels toward the family he is abandoning.

Some men secretly siphon off funds from their joint bank accounts for a few months before departing. Some make off with the family car (or one of the family cars) and all of the family savings. Some are very meticulous: as best they can, they divide the family's savings and other liquid assets in half, almost as if making a financial settlement with their wives. Some leave with only their credit cards and their last paychecks.

But of course there is a minority of men that runs off

almost impulsively. Such men are driven not only by worries but by blind panic; all they know is they *can't take it any more*. So it was with a smartly dressed man looking somewhat disheveled and fatigued, stale whiskey on his breath, who showed up at the Travelers Aid station at Philadelphia International Airport one day in the spring of 1976. Who was he? A career military officer. Why did he run? "I've had all I can take of my wife's drinking," he told the Travelers Aid caseworker.

It turned out that he'd run away as abruptly, as blindly, as a grown man can. His departure followed a fight, their thousandth. As usual, she was drunk; he, enraged. Suddenly, this time, it was different. A peculiar, panicky feeling came over him — the feeling that if he didn't get away immediately he'd fall apart, his limbs would drop off, his torso disintegrate. This feeling so unnerved and frightened him that he ran at once — without anything, even leaving behind his credit cards, taking only a few bills he had at home. With the money he bought a ticket to Philadelphia and drank all night. Now here he was in harsh daylight, sobering up, broke, hoping to wire his parents for more cash, exhausted, bitter, furious, repelled by the notion of returning home but without any concrete idea of what to do.

When amenable to it, such "panic runners" are counseled extensively by Travelers Aid of Philadelphia — sometimes for as many as six hours intermittently throughout the day — to help them arrive at a decision about where to go from there. But few want anything to do with counseling. They want a bed and a stake, and then they want to move on — just move on and on, losing themselves in movement as they might in drink.

While relatively few men run so impulsively, a great many figuratively (some literally) kiss wife and children good-bye in the morning, head for work — and never return home for supper. Some leave notes, many men do not. Abandoning

someone is more than a cry for help, after all; like suicide, it
is also an exquisite form of revenge.

The man who vanishes because of rage toward his wife may
let his mind play lovingly over her reactions to his disappearance; he may go over the likely possibilities, construct a
scenario as a master playwright does a script. At first, when
he doesn't show up for supper, she may not be worried.
(Certainly not if he has had a history of not always showing
up on time, or if he occasionally went boozing with the boys,
or once in a while stayed out all night long.)

But as hour after hour passes, her anxiety grows. She begins
to make ever more frantic phone calls, to friends, relatives,
people at his place of work. Hours more, then a day, a day
and a half with no word from him or from anyone who knows
him. She's atremble with fear, with concern. She calls the
police, enlists a friend's help, calls all the hospitals. She
imagines all kinds of ugly things — he's had an accident, is
lying helpless in a gutter, at the bottom of a ravine. Her mind
depicts situations each more terrible than the last. "He's
been stabbed, shot, hit by a car — he's dead." She cries;
wrenching, hysterical sobs come out of her. Such sweet revenge. *It serves her right, the bitch!*

In time, finally, when nothing is turned up, little bits and
pieces fall into place. The new thought, the terrible thought,
occurs to her. At first she tries to put it out of her mind. It
couldn't be, it's unbelievable. She'd rather think he's been
kidnapped, slain, dropped in the lake in a chunk of cement,
than acknowledge this grim and awful fact — that he's
abandoned her. He thrills to that notion, to the notion of her
ultimate fear.

But then, through his self-pitying rage and vengefulness, a
stray thought enters his consciousness; though he wants to
reject it, it takes form, laser-like, to burn him — *what if she
doesn't give a good goddam?*

So, sooner or later, he telephones. He wants to connect

with home; too, he wants to feed on the concern he hopes she feels. (Will desperation show in her voice?) He may also call one of his relatives to find out how his wife is taking things and to establish another link with his past. According to private detectives who get paid to track down runaway husbands, many such men share their runaway plans with a trusted relative or friend before they take off; this person is the one most likely to receive an early call.

Where They Go

There are men who run away without ever leaving their geographical areas, or even their jobs. Showing lavish trust in their fellow workers, they go to work each day at the same old place. For them it is life as usual, except for the minor fact of having fled from home. The runaway's wife may check with his office or his plant, but she doesn't necessarily get anywhere.

"Lots of times people on the job cover up effectively for the deserting husband, so she still doesn't know where he is," says J. M. Martin, a Manhattan-based private investigator whose specialty it is to track down missing persons.

One runaway husband — call him Abe — has been living comfortably in Brooklyn for the past two years, just a borough away from Queens and the home he and his wife occupied there for twelve years. Abe still faithfully performs his duties at the same tool-and-die shop where he has been employed for nearly a decade. "Those are a great bunch of guys," he boasts. "They'd never give me away. Besides, they know what the situation is."

The situation, he insists, is that he and his wife were talking divorce and she was unfairly trying to hang him up for a lot of alimony. In any event, when he first disappeared his wife came to the shop three or four times to check up on him. Whenever she did, fellow workers tipped him off and he fled out the back door until she left. When she questioned the other men, including the foreman, they cheerfully lied their heads off. "Abe, that *mamzer*, hasn't shown his head around here for weeks." Abe's wife was no dummy; on at least a couple of occasions she hung around outside the shop at closing time, hoping to catch him. But each time she was spotted and Abe fled out the back again.

Most runaway husbands do of course put more distance between themselves and their homes. A relatively small number stays with relatives or friends, people they can count on not to give them away. A few run home to mama. As Harry N. Zelinka, district director of Family Service of Los Angeles, puts it, "Some run back to mama because their wives no longer want to be mama." This is an observation of no little importance to an understanding of many male runaways.

Lots of runaways hit the trail; they want to put great distances between themselves and what for the moment they see as their former lives. East Coast runaways are very apt to head for California. As for Californians, many don't want to leave the state, just their wives, so if they live in Los Angeles, they head for cities like San Diego or San Francisco, and vice versa. Other men, California-made not California-born, return to their home towns in other states.

If runaway husbands don't get jobs and don't go back home they become drifters once their money or credit runs out — sad, embittered skid row types who flee from one form of unhappiness to another. When runaway husbands have specific and marketable trades — if, say, they're plumbers or mechanics or electricians — they tend to pursue that trade wherever they are.

And white-collar husbands? Initially they're less apt to stay in their own occupations. They don't possess a job passport, the union card. Then, too, in reaction to their own dissatisfactions they tend to think that happiness lies in getting one's hands dirty. This helps to explain why runaway husbands who used to be corporation executives are now driving cabs, pumping gas, working on a construction team, doing handy-man jobs. When those executive hands get too dirty and begin to smart, blue-collar verve often loses its staying power. Back they go to white-collar jobs.

Changing Identities

Many of the runaways who show up at Travelers Aid offices asking for help use phony names. Some are ashamed of having run away and don't want to be found out. Some are suspicious of establishment agencies. Some try to get dupli-cate services from the same agency under several names. This has happened so often at the Travelers Aid Society of Wash-ington, D.C., that now this agency refuses to provide any service — except a night's emergency shelter — without verifying the prospective client's identity.

Using a phony name on the spur of the moment is one thing, creating a whole new identity for oneself is another. Despite their fantasies of starting fresh, of going on to lead completely different lives as "new" persons, the vast majority of runaway husbands keep themselves pretty much as they are. Private detectives who look for runaway husbands say that even when such husbands do change their names, they generally won't make drastic changes. Thus, a man who was born John Ray Smith and grew up using John Smith may turn himself into Ray Smith when he runs away, hardly a striking transformation. From a practical viewpoint, a com-plete name change poses some obvious practical difficulties, such as getting work in one's own field of expertise.

But it is not only the practical aspects that keep more run-away husbands from turning Smith into Jones. "Most adults do think of changing identities, and most get discouraged because there's a paranoia that goes with running away," notes Ed Goldfader, president of Tracers Company of America, a leading investigative firm in the missing persons field. "What goes on in the runaway's head is this: there's no real point in running unless somebody cares. He presumes that in running he has disrupted a whole universe back there. He imagines — hopes — that he's initiated all sorts of procedures to find him. He hopes — he feels — that everybody's looking for him. It's easy to get new identification, but he has to get a new Social Security card, and he's afraid to go in and apply because he thinks all sorts of people are waiting to grab him the moment he walks in the door. He never walks down the street without looking over his shoulder, without seeing the reflections in store windows. He thinks the whole world must be out looking for him. I've had firsthand testimony of this from runaway husbands that I've found."

Of course, paranoia runs higher in some runaways than in some others. In any event, it's apt to subside as time goes on and nobody actually tries to make a grab for the runaway. It is the uncommon wife who sends a professional search party out to look for the missing husband. Even if she wants to bother — and she may not — private detectives don't come cheap. And people don't go to a Sam Spade as readily as they do to a doctor, a lawyer, or even a psychiatrist.

As for those men who want to remake themselves into something other than they were, they soon discover that changing identities may be far easier than it seems on a practical level, but far harder emotionally. The man who is determined to start his runaway life fresh and phony must, first of all, make an ironclad compact with himself. It is a compact to the effect that he will not tell a single living soul about his runaway plans.. Unless he has the tight-lipped gambler's mentality, this may be the toughest part. To leave without saying a word to another soul is extremely hard. To be away and to refrain from making contact with anyone — relative, friend, colleague, anyone at all from one's past — is just as hard. As one man who succeeded at it mused, "It's like engineering your death and your rebirth, all by yourself."

Another vital move for the man who wants to run away

and change himself is to take nothing with him that could be traced. His car, his credit cards, his union card, his library card, his checks, his bankbooks — he must leave them all behind. Otherwise, if someone is determined to find him, just one of the artifacts of his past is likely to give him away.

There are don'ts, there are dos in creating a new identity. The runaway *does* need to fill his empty wallet with a whole new set of credentials. The basis for them all is a brand-new birth certificate with the name he intends to adopt. People determined to do this go to their local libraries or newspaper offices and get hold of newspapers published around the time of their own births or a few years later. They examine the obituary columns to find obituaries of same-sex persons born in approximately the same year they were but who died as young children. This information can also be gotten in the death certificate register in the county recorder's office. The important thing for the runaway determined to become a new person is to find someone who, had he not died young, would now be roughly the same age as the prospective runaway.

But why not simply get the birth certificate of someone who died recently? Because such people actually reached adulthood, and as a result have histories, have left a trail of official papers in their wake. Young children have had no Social Security numbers or other potentially embarrassing evidences of the longer lived life. The runaway doesn't want to risk embarrassment. He simply wants to "steal" the dead child's name and parlay it into that new identity.

Once he has found a name he orders a copy of that deceased person's birth certificate from the appropriate state bureau of vital statistics. It's a chore the federal government has simplified through its 35-cent publication, *Where to Write for Birth and Death Records,* which gives a rundown on both where to write and what to pay.

So now he has not only a new name but "proof" that he is

who he says he is. That's all he needs in order to apply for a new magic number, a Social Security number. (Proof of age isn't needed for persons under eighteen who are born in the United States or Puerto Rico.) A few years ago Social Security offices were lax about demanding proof of age; now things have tightened up considerably. However, regional variations still exist. Social Security offices in the New York City area are among the strictest in the nation in terms of requiring documentation. Nevertheless, usually even middle-aged men and women who apply for new Social Security cards, possibly having presented manufactured proof of age, aren't asked how it is that they've lived this long without one. If they are asked, and reply, "Because I've never worked before," in most instances the low-echelon clerks who do the interviewing aren't likely to pursue the question. Proof of age is enough. Of course, the fleeing husband leaves himself open to a year in prison, a fine of $1,000, or both, if he's discovered.

Once in possession of his Social Security number, his precious identification number, the runaway can open a bank account, fill out an employment application, and eventually pay the income taxes he'll be owing as he pursues his new life. If the running gets tough, he can also use the number to apply for welfare. As for his new birth certificate, it's the tool that will fashion for him a passport and a driver's license. In these ways he pyramids his credentials and fleshes out his new identity.

Since everything can be commercialized, even new identities, there exists a thriving phony ID industry, involving identity brokers who peddle lists of dead persons and instructional materials on how to use them, sellers of fake ID cards and merchants of stolen passports and driver's licenses. Illegal aliens, fugitives from the law, con men and credit skips are the main purchasers of such items, but a few runaway men take advantage of them, too. A federal task force has been looking into the phony ID problem. Many concerned observers feel that the only way to resolve the most widespread abuses is by computer-linking birth and death certificates — a costly operation.

Actually, few runaway men avail themselves of false IDs. Few make a massive effort at radical transformation of self. One reason is fear; runaways are not criminals and such maneuvers are wholly alien to them. Another reason they keep on using their old names and living their lives in the old familiar way as much as possible is that basically they don't mean to make as sharp a break with their past as running might suggest. Many, probably most, runaway husbands want eventually to be taken by the hand and led back home. Many, if not most, want to be discovered.

At any rate, that is the assessment of a number of social workers and private detectives who come into professional contact with these men. Their reasoning is based on the fact that these runaways are too careless. They leave too many clues — using their old credit cards, for instance, and "forgetting" that duplicate slips will be sent to their homes. They're like cheating spouses who leave clues to their infidelities in hopes of being found out.

Passage Home

So, sooner or later most runaway husbands find that the adventure begins to pall. They come to the reluctant realization that their new lives aren't as glamorous or rewarding as they had fantasized. They're lonely. Nostalgic thoughts of home steal over them. They think of their children, their wives, their friends. A subtle shift occurs in their mental outlook — from running away to running back. More and more of their fantasies have to do with going home. How will my wife receive me? What will my children say? Their calls home, midnight or otherwise, increase. They begin dialogues with their abandoned wives, or, before communicating directly, call friends and ask them for an assessment of the climate back home. In these and other ways they begin the delicate emotional negotiations that precede a return.

Obviously, not everybody who runs fits into this neat pattern. There are men who never show up again. There are men who do carve new and happier lives for themselves, at which point they usually make contact with their wives, either in person or through an attorney, to arrange for a divorce. There are men who disappear one day, let nothing be heard of themselves for years, then suddenly reappear on the steps of the old homestead.

In Memphis a family man kissed his wife and two young sons good-bye; he was off on a hunting trip with his bird dogs, his beloved shotgun and a load of shells. He failed to return home. For twenty-nine years nothing was heard from him. Then, as abruptly as he had left, he showed up again. He gave one short explanation for his disappearance to his wife: "Guess I just wanted to get around."

7

Runaway Wives: Fear, Frustration and Fantasy

Sudden Departure

Facing each other in the family service social worker's sparsely furnished cubicle, this wife and husband showed a gamut of difficult emotions on their faces. Hurt, torment, regret, love. He was incredulous. She was adamant. He talked about how much they had gone through together to lick their drinking problems. She said she'd conquered hers but that he was still drinking. He said yes, but not as much. She said it made no difference, she was leaving him. He invoked history, their early happier years, the fun they'd had together as teenagers, the good sex, their teenage wedding. She told him that that was a long time ago, that now they had two teenage sons of their own. Yes, he said, yes, they had two children, two good boys, they needed to stay together as a family. As gently as she could, and with a sparkle of tears in her eyes, she replied that right now she had important needs of her own.

At that he could no longer suppress his anger. Out came a stream of invective against the women's movement; he carried on with special bitterness about the consciousness-raising group to which she'd belonged for a while. She remained calm, looked at him with a hint of contempt, said it was exactly that kind of attitude which had a lot to do with why she wanted to leave. She went on in that vein, said he didn't really understand her, said he couldn't get it through his head how important certain things were to her now, said how necessary it was for her to find herself as a person.

Seeking the words that would slay the dragon, he said yes, the whole thing had really started — the change in her had begun — when she stopped being a housewife and got herself a job in a dental office. It was the beginning of their downhill slide; it was when she started having those strange ideas. She demanded: Is going on the wagon and getting a job and discovering that you're a capable person after all really that strange? He shifted the argument: But right along, all these years, I loved you. She opened her mouth to respond, but he interrupted. I loved you, he repeated. I'm not the kind of guy who falls on his knees and recites poetry or something, but I loved you and bought you a house and a car and everything you needed.

Her voice breaking just a little, she acknowledged that, in his own way, he did love her. Having said that enabled her to regain control and she went on: she told him she'd suddenly realized that being loved didn't mean being taken care of, it meant being *responded* to. He shook his head the way a person does when he suddenly finds his life, the life he thought he knew so well, foreign and menacing. Softly she begged him to understand. He shook his head again, said again how he'd given her everything — a nice home, good food, long vacations; he reminded her that he worked hard, twelve hours a day, to provide for his family; then he shouted *I've given you me*. And her short, stunning reply was, *No, you haven't*. And then their counseling hour was up.

Two weeks later, when he came home from work, she was gone. The children were gone. Some of the furniture and all of the personal effects belonging to her and the boys were gone. His heart pounding, he began to bang on doors in their quiet little neighborhood of tract houses now being reddened by the setting southern California sun. A neighbor told him about the moving van that had pulled up earlier in the day and how all the stuff had been loaded aboard and how his wife and the boys had then driven away.

For a month he didn't know where she was. She came to the family service agency for treatment, for support. He came in for treatment, for support, hoping to run into her, but of course this husband and wife had now been scheduled for different days. When his runaway wife finally did contact him it was to tell him she was filing for divorce.

Why So Many Run

When one asks social service and private detective agencies about new developments in relation to runaways, the answer is usually the same: "It's the women, the wives. In recent years there's been a sharp upsurge in wives who run away from home."

A telling statistic from Tracers Company of America: in 1969 just 2 percent of the runaway spouses the company was asked to track down were women. By 1971 the number had jumped to 42 percent. In 1975 the company was looking for more wives than husbands.

"There seems to be a dramatic increase in the number of wives running from intolerable situations," notes F. Stowe Hull from his vantage point at the Travelers Aid Society of Philadelphia.

What a wife sees as an intolerable situation, her husband

may not. This was clearly evident in the case of that runaway wife in southern California. The husband couldn't tolerate her change, she couldn't tolerate his lack of toleration.

Many of the wives who run are in the same predicament. They're in their late twenties or thirties or forties. Usually as a result of therapy or the women's movement they're facing themselves and their worlds in a new way. Involved in the turmoil and torment that bespeaks inner struggle, they see themselves as victims of emotional neglect. Beyond that broad generality, perspectives vary. Some want their husbands to pay more attention to them, to be more loving. Some feel their husbands have been treating them like children; now they rebel against having been dependent all their lives, first on their fathers, then on their husbands. Some feel that, with increasing age and maturity, they've grown far beyond their husbands. Many have pleaded for years with their husbands to make some changes, and have been steadfastly ignored, before they run. And when they go, many of them, they hope that their dramatic absence will bring about the changes that their pleading presences did not.

Many runaway wives leave homes in which talk is small talk or abstract talk rather than emotional talk — homes in which feelings are rarely explored. Many have husbands who do work hard, who are successful in terms of their breadwinning role, but who validate themselves as husbands and fathers almost wholly by how much money they bring in or by how much they offer their families materially.

"We always had lots of food and we lived in a nice house; Harry was a good provider," said Betty, the runaway wife of a factory foreman in Michigan. "But after dinner he'd watch TV and on weekends he'd do something with his buddies. He never wanted to talk to me, just sit down on the couch together and talk. He'd say, 'What's there to talk about? Talk to the kids, talk to your girlfriends — women love to rattle on a mile a minute.' He just couldn't see what I wanted."

"He couldn't see what I wanted" and "He couldn't see *me*"

are the complaints so often voiced by discontented wives who finally run away. Indeed, many newly deserted husbands haven't "seen" their wives in years. Men who hire Tracers to find their missing mates are frequently vague when they are asked specific questions about them. They may have lived with these women for fifteen years or so, yet do not know the color of their eyes, what kinds of foods they like best, what sports and hobbies they enjoy most.

Nor do they seem to have had any inkling of the seriousness of their marital problems. As Ron Johnson of the Family and Children's Service of Minneapolis says, "The man's message often is, 'Yeah, well, we had problems but they didn't seem that serious to me.' They're stuck for the reason why they've been abandoned. But real deterioration was going on for some time and they shut their eyes to it."

Men whose wives abandon them after a period of discontent often blame Women's Liberation for things. They like to say the movement has poisoned their wives' minds. They forget that while the movement may indeed put a woman's frustrations into sharp focus, those frustrations were already there and the rage they produced had been expressed, albeit circuitously, right along. Too, it seems self-evident that as women gain more education, more awareness, more sophisticated job skills and a greater potential for careers, they come to expect more satisfactions for themselves. What could be more human?

Sometimes Running Is Easier

It is only human to expect one's frustrations to be resolved, one's needs to be met. But if they aren't, why pack up and run away? Why not face the issue squarely and, if necessary, begin legitimate separation and divorce proceedings?

The answer for many runaway wives is that they aren't sufficiently sure of themselves — not yet, anyway — in terms

of their newfound assertiveness. As Betty, the Michigan foreman's wife, put it, "Well, if I hadn't taken off the way I did,
Harry might have talked me into staying."

Yes, she had her ambivalences. And she knew she was still
vulnerable to Harry's entreaties, to the pressures he would
inevitably apply. Here was a push-pull battle between dependence and independence, one she realized she would be
unable to resolve with Harry on the scene. For the moment,
at least, the only thing she felt herself capable of doing to
help herself was to steal away in the middle of the night.

There are many Bettys.

And some wives run because, at the moment, running seems
easier than facing a dreaded ordeal of confrontation, con-
tested divorce and child custody actions. The wives feel
panicky, feel they simply can't go through the experience. So
they take off. If they're lucky, or if they seek counseling and
it works, in time they marshal their energies enough to return
home and do what has to be done.

Leaving with Lovers

Many runaway wives do not leave alone, they leave with
men — but not necessarily because they're madly in love with
their lovers. They may think they're in love, but their boyfriends really provide them with the structure and support
they need in order to desert.

So it was with Paulette, a secretary in her late twenties. She
and her husband were childless. She described her husband as
a "sweet bore" and as a man afflicted with a serious sexual
problem — premature ejaculation — for which he refused to
get help. She knew she had to leave him but whenever she
brought up the subject of a separation he "fell apart."

According to Paulette, "He just couldn't face the prospect
so I always got sidetracked."

She obviously allowed herself to get sidetracked, yet still

wanted to leave. So she began an affair with a married man, one of the salesmen in her office. Unlike her husband, this man was rugged-looking, with a macho swagger, and very exciting in bed. They talked about running away together. While they spent weeks negotiating this, the salesman's wife took more direct action; she left him. Whereupon he urged Paulette to move in with him at once. After yet another anguished scene with her husband, she stuffed some clothes into a suitcase and settled in with her lover one weekend while her husband was visiting his sick mother. She didn't even leave a note. But within two weeks she had tired of this man and his pompous, pushy ways, and got herself a small apartment. She planned to stay alone for a while until she got a clearer sense of herself and of what she wanted to do.

Allowing for minor variations, Paulette's pattern of running isn't unusual. A social worker at the Family Service of Los Angeles reflected on her caseload of runaway wives and said, "I've worked with a number of women runaways who wanted to leave home and waited for some opportunity to occur. They find themselves men who become that opportunity, who become that last pressure they need to enable them to make the break. Often these men are quite different from their husbands and totally unsuited to them. The relationship doesn't develop, but the purpose is served. The women quite unconsciously create these situations."

Some runaway wives leave with men, others leave with women. Some observers of the current sociosexual scene say the incidence of lesbianism and bisexuality has increased; some say it is just more apparent. Whatever the truth, therapists and other professionals who come in contact with runaway wives say they're seeing more wives taking off to be with women they love. Often these wives are mothers with preteen children; occasionally they take their youngsters with them to be part of their new family.

Husbands tend to be much more upset if their wives run away with other women than if they go with other men.

They can understand old-fashioned playing around — but *my* wife, the woman *I* married, a *lesbian*? It is just as upsetting to a man as it is to a woman when her husband is discovered with a male lover rather than a female one. They react as if somehow their own sexuality has been violated.

When a woman runs off with another woman it can also foster more violence on the part of the deserted husband than if she left with a man, especially if there are children involved. A case handled by the Brooklyn Bureau of Community Service vividly illustrates the point. Arlene, the wife in this situation, had left to live with a close woman friend, taking her two children with her. The husband and father, Sal, wanted her back. As he saw things initially, Arlene was under the evil influence of her girlfriend, who'd poisoned her mind against him.

Then the case became complicated by the fact that Sal had several conversations with the girlfriend's husband, Gino; the two deserted men became good friends. Gino knew about their wives' sexual relationship, however, and told Sal. A violent argument between the two men and two women ensued. Next, the two women and Sal's children disappeared. At that, Sal almost literally made it his life's goal to find Arlene and get his youngsters back. Several months went by, during which time he persisted in questioning and requestioning her friends and relatives. Finally he learned that the four of them had gone to Hawaii. He promptly flew to Honolulu and confronted the two women. There was an angry argument; he stormed out. When he returned the next day they were gone again. He has not seen them since and is presumably still hunting for them.

Battered Wives

Many of the wives who run away do so because their husbands beat them or because the threat of being battered is ever-present in their lives. Some have been brutalized for years and finally have had enough. Others go when their children are also in danger of being beaten. They take the younger ones but sometimes leave the older children, who presumably are better able to take care of themselves, behind.

Obvious question: Why don't these wives go to the police instead of running?

Obvious answer: Because all too frequently police officers and family courts give them no help. In fact, in December 1976 activist lawyers in New York City filed a unique suit — one asking the police department and the Family Court to obey *existing laws* with respect to abused wives.

Another question: Why don't the women simply take their children and openly and legally split from their violence-prone husbands?

Answer: Because they still wouldn't be safe from possible mayhem.

According to Judith Carlin, director of Family Location and Legal Services, an arm of New York City's Jewish Family Service: "Sometimes the only way to go is underground, because some husbands are literally crazy. While the wife can get an order of protection from the court, it won't do any good. She just has to disappear."

Consider a typical case, a tragic case, in which Ms. Carlin was involved. A husband with a history of wife-beating was in prison on an unrelated charge. As the day of his release approached he called his wife from prison threatening to kill her when he got out. She wanted an order of protection. The court refused to issue her one as long as the man was still incarcerated. Ms. Carlin could have obtained one for this terror-stricken wife on the day of his release, but a piece of paper would hardly have stopped him from going after her. And since the document would list her address, he would immediately know where she was living if she simply moved to another address. So this particular wife had no choice but to take her children and disappear in a nearby state. She achieved a measure of safety for herself and for her children, but at considerable sacrifice — having to hide and forfeiting any chance of getting child support.

In this instance it was perfectly legal for the wife to vanish with her children. It isn't always. Not, for instance, if the battered wife is separated or divorced from the man who used to beat her but who has visitation rights. What then? Then, Ms. Carlin observes, "She has to make a conscious choice about what's best for her and the children. The proper thing would be for her to go to court and testify how terrible the man is, and have the visitation rights modified."

Proper, maybe — but many of the battered wives, as a result of cruel personal experience, have little faith left in the humanity or the effectiveness of the courts. Besides, they know full well that even if visitation rights were denied, their angry ex-husbands could still crash in and lay violent hands on them and on their children. So those who can, manage to move to another state — visitation rights be damned. In any event, most states do not have reciprocity in terms of visitation rights or custody orders, though ten have already adopted a Uniform Child Custody Act that has been in the works since 1968.

Planners and Fantasists

Like their counterparts, the runaway husbands, runaway wives vary in how they actually run. Some meticulously save nickels, dimes and quarters until they feel they have enough money to tide them over the initial weeks. Alice is one such wife; with her husband teetering on the edge of alcoholism and her teenage son getting harder and harder to handle, she carefully put away odd sums left over at the end of the month when the bills were paid. It took her over a year to do it, but when she had $500 saved up she ran.

Some other wives make careful plans ahead of time, arranging as precisely as they can where they'll go and what they'll do; many such women have access to joint bank accounts they can dip into upon departure. Barbara is among these runaways. The beautiful wife of a successful stockbroker, his showpiece, the mother of three demanding children, she took off only a few hours before she was to entertain at one of the many lavish parties her husband loved to throw. When she left she took $50,000 from their joint savings account. When she resurfaced, several months later, she would have nothing further to do with her husband or her children.

On the whole, runaway wives more than husbands are apt to leave messages behind. How they do varies from person to person. A few relay messages through friends. Some leave fairly terse, though emotional, notes — one read, "I had to go, I love you, love the children, don't look for me, I'm not coming back." Some are notes of desperation, some carry a mixed tone of profound anger and profound sadness. There are women who spell out in precise detail why they left, as though making one final effort to reach their husbands.

Though on the whole runaway wives are more careful planners than runaway husbands, many do run more or less impulsively. At best they have vague plans for the future. Their heads are filled with fantasies — bits and pieces of hope for a better life. *I'll get a job. I'll meet a guy, handsome and rich, who'll take me to Europe on a fling. I'll get myself a small studio and sculpt. I'll live communally with loving sisters. I'll go to California and lie in the sun and something good will happen to me. My husband will be so sorry to see me gone. He'll come right after me, beg forgiveness, and then everything will be all right.*

But few such impulse runners can turn lovely fantasy into satisfying reality. Few find jobs, except maybe very menial ones like changing sheets in a cheap motel. If they meet men at all, they are men who tend to be as unstable as themselves — or shrewdly exploitative. Most women refugees, with little or no money and little or no talent, find the life of the artist beyond them. A small minority is lucky enough to end up in communal arrangements with sympathetic women, but sometimes they tend to be so hurt, so angry and needy, that their new alliances don't last long. Some go to California, where the sun *is* warm, but they soon discover that ripe fruit does not, by magic, plop into their mouths. And their husbands are not apt to come after them transformed into knights in shining armor.

For all of this, the number of wives who run on impulse seems to be growing, according to Samuel Mopsik, director of Field Service for Travelers Aid International–Social Service of America. Mopsik's work takes him to Travelers Aid offices all over the country, and many have been reporting an increasingly common pattern — young runaway wives who engage in "unplanned movement."

"Typically," Mopsik says, "such a wife breaks the piggy bank, takes the youngest child or two, goes to the bus line and uses the money to buy a ticket to the farthest place she can. She ends up somewhere without a penny and contacts Travelers Aid."

And she obviously has some immediate, imperative problems: a need for food and shelter, a means of taking care of her young children, her shaky emotional self. Her shakiness may be intensified by a numbing fear, as well — that a social agency to which she goes for help will declare her an unfit mother and attempt to take her children from her.

Some runaway wives walk an emotional tightrope and face a growing danger of falling off. Among them are those who were not very well-balanced to begin with and for whom daily life in unhappy family circumstances has intensified their instability.

Because of the way they were raised and socialized in a male-dominated society, many runaway wives are helpless in the face of the demands being made upon them as fugitives. They are not at all prepared for these demands. How is a woman who hasn't worked in fifteen years, and who has little that's impressive in the way of education or job skills, going to support herself and the children with whom she has fled? How is a woman who has for her entire life relied on male figures going to manage alone?

There is a painful paradox at hand for the woman who runs away. On the one hand, the imperatives of survival require her to be as clever, as responsible, as competent, as she can be. On the other hand, she's in danger of falling apart as she tries to pursue her life on the road. Yet if she had kept on facing the daily traumas at home she *would* have fallen apart; instinctive awareness of that fact is at least partly what prompted her to run away in the first place. Finally, though, running becomes even harder than staying. Professionals knowledgeable in the ways of runaway wives say that roughly half return home within a few weeks — or are so careless about hiding that they're easily found.

Patterns of Survival

What's the modus operandi of those runaway wives who try to plan, who do not just suddenly break open the piggy bank and take off? Where do they go? What do they do? Some run to friends who are sympathetic to their plight, but frequently friends can provide only temporary refuge. Some run to relatives, but for one reason or another, relatives aren't always sympathetic. A Travelers Aid volunteer working in an East Coast airport recalled an incident involving a young wife. The volunteer had come upon her crying in a corner of the airport, near a bank of telephones. She had run — yet again — from her physically abusive husband. Though she was a college graduate and had worked as an administrative assistant at one time, she seemed strikingly lost and helpless.

Whenever she'd run away from her husband in the past, her parents, who lived in a Philadelphia suburb, had helped her. But they had also been insistent that she finally leave her husband. She hadn't done so; she couldn't. This time, in response to her plea for help, they'd said, "No, we've had enough." She didn't know what to do, where to turn. Travelers Aid helped her get housing and a job and referred her to a local family service agency for long-term counseling.

Many observers believe that because women have more access to money and jobs, their own cars, more freedom to move, more of a say in their own lives generally than in the past, they find it easier to survive on the road. That's true — up to a point. Even today, though, a great many women's lives are still characterized by patterns of subservience and dependency. Too, in some respects that cold, harsh world out there is even harsher to runaway wives than it is to their male counterparts. For instance, in major cities like Los Angeles, down-and-out runaway husbands can always find a flophouse or a mission bed to plunk down in. That's not true in the case of runaway wives. In fact, because of the dearth of emergency shelters for women, social service agencies like Travelers Aid sometimes have trouble finding beds for destitute and near-destitute women.

For the runaway wife who needs to watch every dime, YWCAs are one solution. Many end up in cheap rooming houses for a time. Free clinics — for instance, the Los Angeles Free Clinic — usually have a list of available crash pads, but this approach generally occurs only to women brought up in the counterculture movement. Another approach that occurs to relatively few runaway wives is to tap the women's movement as a resource. Many major cities now have women's centers that provide services to women generally. The Women's Building in Los Angeles; the National Organization for Women (NOW) chapters in New York City and elsewhere; Casa de los Madres, a refuge for battered wives in San Francisco, are all examples. Some of these centers do help runaway wives, and some Travelers Aid agencies refer such women to them.

In fact, in response to the need, there has sprung up an informal network of refuges for runaway wives in many metropolitan centers. Individual, concerned feminists volunteer their own homes as temporary crash pads for runaway wives who have no place to stay. Some of the women's centers, which don't like to talk about this facet of their operations (maybe because they don't want to be inundated, or don't want to seem to be encouraging wives to run away), act as informal clearing houses to bring together the homeless women and the women who offer their homes.

As for work, if a woman has a job skill she may be able to parlay it into good-paying work when she is on the run — at least work that provides her with enough income so she can gain a little breathing space and figure out what to do next with her life. Of course, if she is too depressed or agitated, no amount of skill will help her get or hold on to a job. Some runaway wives, looking for a freedom they failed to find at home, finally are forced into menial, boring or physically exhausting jobs. As one private detective says, "They'll take any kind of job they can get. They'll become waitresses, motel maids — filler-time jobs where they don't take out any taxes."

Many work as salesgirls, clerks, receptionists. An executive's wife became a restaurant hostess; some shapely runaway wives turn up in topless and bottomless joints, temporarily gyrating their way through life. A few begin to work as prostitutes, both as a way of maintaining themselves and as a further expression of rebelliousness. So it was with a minister's wife from Atlanta; she fled to Chicago, spent six months as a whore, then returned home and filed for divorce.

Men certainly do not have a monopoly on either the act of skipping out or the adolescent fantasies that often fuel their departures. Nor is it only male runaways who try to lose themselves in drinking bouts and sexual adventures and drugs. Wives, too, try to run away from themselves even as they become runaways; they, too, have delicious fantasies to which they try to give life.

Thus a fair number of the runaways wind up in California, symbol of all that's bright and shiny and *hopeful* — hoping to be discovered as movie stars, as TV performers, as singers and models. (There's no place like California — especially Los Angeles — for the acting out of fantasies.) Some wind up for a time with the small bands of communards in Topanga Canyon or settle into tiny beach apartments in Venice, to loll on the beach and make it with the bronzed young boys.

Yet for every runaway wife who soaks up the southern California sun there are numerous others who don't even approach such lotus-eating. Instead, they live in drab, decaying rooming houses, work at humdrum jobs, drink in neighborhood bars, meet the kinds of men it's hard to fantasize about, or meet nobody at all and nurse their acute cases of loneliness, wondering when something good will ever happen to them.

What about the Children?

Women with young children, whose husbands are abusive, usually run with the kids. Women approaching or in middle age, whose children are already in their middle teens or older, are less likely to take them — though if there are young children in the family, they occasionally take them along.

Runaway wives with children have the hardest time finding emergency housing, jobs (with the dearth of day-care centers, who's going to take care of the kids all day long?) and members of the opposite sex (how are you going to meet men if you have a couple of demanding youngsters to look after?). Wives who take their children may qualify for Aid to Dependent Children, and the women's centers or social service agencies will help them get it. If they leave their young ones

behind they're physically more mobile but emotionally more
burdened; it's hard not to feel some guilt.

"I was a rotten mother, I know, and I didn't want to be
around them," recalls Jane, an alcoholic who went on periodic
binges and who learned to stay dry only after she had left
home. "I knew their father would take good care of them.
But this motherhood thing is so strong. When you're still a
little girl they begin stuffing you with it. Even though I knew
I was doing everyone a favor, I still felt like I'd committed
the crime of the century. It was so illogical. I was a lousy
mother but I kept thinking how I'd let them down by leaving — when the fact is, I let them down every day I was with
them."

Another runaway mother described these attacks of guilt
as "just like time bombs — thought I'd explode."

Mothers who seem to fare best overall as runaways are
those who take their kids along but who were fully in charge
of their households even before they left — competent women
forced to hold their families together both economically and
emotionally. A thirty-two-year-old mother in Detroit brought
her two children to California, leaving her husband uncere-
moniously because "he was the laziest slob in the world."
She said he hated to work and lost every job he ever got. As
for herself — "I supported him from the day we married. I
don't remember a bill he ever paid, and he hardly ever did
anything around the house, either." She has a good-paying
secretarial job and for the time being would just as soon keep
her status as runaway wife. She plans never to marry again.

Coming Home

Like runaway husbands, wives who abandon their families
also feel the need to maintain contact with home. But they're
less apt to be "breathers" who simply listen to a mate's or a
child's voice without responding. More likely, they engage

in quick, tearful, hurting exchanges. One wife, ultimately tracked down by a Los Angeles detective, telephoned her husband every day for weeks from a Fort Worth phone booth; it was her pattern of steady calls that finally enabled him to find her in Texas.

Of course, there are wives who establish new lives for themselves in distant places and are never heard from again. But just as the majority of husbands want to be found, so do most runaway wives. They want to return because it is too tough out there, because they're lonely for home, or because they want to formalize their new status by getting a divorce. They want to return, and many of them want the decision to be made for them. And so, like many of the runaway husbands, they mark their paths with clues that lead to their discovery, or return home on their own after negotiating by phone or letters with their mates.

They return hoping to be wanted, needed, welcomed — hoping that now things will be different. Unfortunately, their hopes aren't often realized. Frequently, reconciliation in the case of both runaway wives and runaway husbands is more bitter than sweet. Like unexorcised ghosts, the couple's old and destructive patterns remain to haunt them. Many end up separating in the traditional manner. In other cases they conclude even before returning home that what they want is a legal separation or divorce. Counseling, perhaps, has brought some order to their disordered lives and thoughts; in a sense they've given themselves "permission" to leave their husbands legitimately.

Running never is a magic cure for ailing marriages, whatever other necessary purposes it may serve. The only medicine that has a chance of working is two people really wanting to make the marriage a success, wanting to change, working very hard to achieve that goal. That's familiar advice — but there's no running away from it.

8

Runaways and Left-behinds: Themes in Common

An Orderly Retreat

When a spouse runs away, the act may mark a point in a continuum of withdrawal. Start with the inevitable misunderstandings and dissatisfactions that arise in any marriage. There are a number of ways to respond to these; one way, a destructive one, is by withdrawing. Withdrawing means denying the other spouse sex, affection, attention, warmth or contact. The next stage in the continuum may involve sulkiness, angry silences. Further along, the spouse in retreat fails to show up for dinner sometimes, or has an affair, or uses psychosomatic illnesses or depression to create more distance in the marital relationship. Still further along the continuum, the withdrawing partner stays with a friend or a relative for a few days ("running home to mother" could fall into this category). Then comes the initial, tentative running-away episode — the prospective runaway does actually take off for a few days, almost as a rehearsal for the real thing. The most extreme point in the continuum is a lengthy runaway period followed by divorce.

Obviously, not all runaway spouses follow this pattern so neatly. Also, when they do, it is unconscious, not something they plan logically and calculatingly. The point is that progressive alienation and withdrawal always precede the act of running away. And running is always an expression of extreme withdrawal; that holds as true for the wife who leaves a note saying, "I love you anyway" as it does for the husband who simply disappears.

In this and in other ways husbands who run from their wives, and wives who run from their husbands, have a lot in common. But, surprising as it may seem, the mate of either sex who runs and the mate who has been abandoned are also very much alike — and in the most startling ways, the ways of personality and background.

Can it really be? Can the emotionally deprived wife who flees from her unfeeling, unempathic husband — can this wife and this husband be alike? Can the physically abused wife and the abusive mate she flees from be alike in certain ways? The debt-laden husband and the pushy wife?

Victim and victimizer — what could they possibly have in common?

Drinkers in the Family

One thing they frequently have in common is alcohol, and what alcohol represents. Many runaway husbands do a lot of drinking while their crisis builds. Often they have reached the heavy drinking stage by the time they leave. Many of the wives who are left behind may not themselves be heavy drinkers but come from homes in which the father drank heavily (and possibly was abusive) and the mother wrung her hands helplessly, passively.

So he drinks a lot, so she comes from a family in which her father drank a lot. In terms of personality, how does that make them alike? Heavy drinkers (of both sexes) need alcohol because without it they can't cope with their environment, without it they become nervous and irritable, feeling inadequate and dependent. Studies of the wives of alcoholics show that though these women may seem strong and energetic, and seem to be holding their families together, underneath they too are insecure, nervous and dependent. In fact, it is their feelings of dependency — of powerlessness and inadequacy — that initially led them to choose husbands even weaker than they. And, often, when their mates ease up on their drinking, these wives engage in a variety of subtle though unconscious behaviors designed to undermine their progress. They become cranky, create scenes, warn others not to serve their husbands alcoholic drinks (despite the resentment this creates in their mates), altogether behave as though wanting to drive their husbands to drink again.

Teenage Marriage

When teenagers marry they may do so because they think they're in love. They may also marry because they're tired of living with their folks, and because it is — or seems — safer to marry than to go completely on one's own into the harsh adult world. They're eager to leave the nest called home, and they fail to see that they're simply going into another nest called marriage, without first undergoing a period of facing life as autonomous adults. Moving from one nest to another is moving from one dependency to another, and there is a price that's paid — a delay of the maturation process.

Mental health professionals who work with families in which one spouse has had a runaway episode report that in a striking number of cases the pair wed as teenagers and married so young because of their intense dependency needs — needs that even as adults they have not ameliorated or resolved.

"We all have dependency needs we want fulfilled, but the level of need changes with maturation," Harry Zelinka of Family Service of Los Angeles points out. "The sixteen-year-old who gets married literally is saying, 'Take care of me.' That goes for the girl in the situation and it goes for the boy, too. He's saying, 'Let me take care of you — but you're really my mother.'"

In order to become a teenage bride a girl may first have to become a teenage mother. And it so happens that not only do a good many wives in runaway-spouse cases marry in their teens, they are pregnant when they do wed.

He marries to be safe; she marries to be safe; she has a baby she dreams will love her and nurture her, as she dreams her husband will love and nurture her. His dream, articulated or denied, is that she will love and nurture him. "Will you take care of me?" is the question that dominates their existence.

A Pattern of Evasion

Marrying should be predicated on the reality of being an independently functioning person. Runaway spouses and their mates usually exhibit a broad pattern of evading reality. They evade it by marrying too young. They evade it with alcohol. They evade it by not coming to grips with their problems, by denying they exist. Then, when it is no longer possible to keep up the pretense, they panic and run.

This is the predicament in which Betsy and Chandler found themselves. In their mid-twenties, this pair could hardly be said to be a shining example of marital happiness. Chandler, the owner of a low-volume gas station, enjoyed sex with his attractive wife but otherwise ignored her. Betsy felt neglected and as emotionally deprived as a child whose parents pay little attention to her. Whenever she brought up the subject, Chandler merely grunted or withdrew into peevish silence. Whereupon she dropped the subject and didn't bring it up again until she couldn't stand it anymore.

Both Chandler and Betsy practiced evasion, Chandler because he didn't want to face a sensitive issue in their lives. He was delighted when Betsy dropped the subject; it enabled him to follow the line of least resistance. As for Betsy, even though she brought up the crucial subject from time to time, *she never followed through.* She wasn't secure enough to do so. Whenever Chandler so much as growled it was enough to keep her from pursuing her point — and with an inner sense of relief, too.

In time Betsy met another man who seemed to her everything Chandler was not; she flung herself into a passionate affair with him. The affair ended abruptly when an outraged Chandler discovered its existence. Hounded by her punishing husband, pressured by the other man, too used to evasion to confront her problems directly, Betsy ran away.

Patterns of Powerlessness

What follows is a typical picture of married life among couples where runaway episodes eventually occur:

He feels let down by her. She feels let down by him. Each can truthfully say, "You're no longer meeting my needs." Often the kids are a factor. When they come, as they grow, she has to pay increasing amounts of time to them and can no longer cater to him as before. He resents that. She feels resentful of being tied down to the home. He stays out longer and longer each night. She feels less and less able to cope with her own unhappiness — or his.

Elaborating on this pattern, Naumi Alcalay of the Brooklyn Bureau of Community Services says, "And when he does come home it's to an argument, or to reproaches, or to a tremendous fight. If this is compounded by financial problems and by some additional demands on the wife's part — 'You're not taking me out, you come home and just watch TV, you don't listen to my troubles' — then he's apt to come home to a house in disarray. His food isn't prepared. Because of his own strong dependency needs he sees his wife partly as a mother who takes care of him, and when she doesn't do so he interprets that as not caring. She doesn't know how to cope with his demands, he doesn't know how to cope with hers. Neither knows how to say 'no' to those demands in a responsible way. So finally the only way out he sees for himself is by getting out."

The theme inherent in this pattern is *powerlessness*. The theme, over and over among runaway-prone couples, and applying as much to the abandoned spouse as to the abandoner, is — yet again — *dependency*.

Everyone has dependency needs that must be satisfied if one is to live a healthy emotional life; their appropriateness hinges on intensity and degree. Highly dependent men and women lack a sense of power over their lives. What is missing is the perception that they have the capacity to deal with and change for the better problematic issues in their lives. When they marry, whether very young or older, they invest their mates with the power they feel they lack. As long as their mate provides it, everything is fine. When the mate seems to fail — and who can "do it all" for the other over a prolonged period of time? — they feel utterly let down.

To feel so powerless is to feel lost and frightened. But this can be too much to bear, too much to face. Thus many very dependent persons deny their dependency needs altogether: to acknowledge them is to risk being overwhelmed by them, so uncontrollable do they seem. Much better, safer, to pretend they don't exist at all. Men, conditioned to see themselves as possessing strengths they can't possibly claim in real life, are especially likely to do this. And when they run away they sometimes reconcile the act of running with their tough-guy visions of themselves by a show of little-boy bravado: they're gaining revenge.

Playing Musical Chairs

If two people have these urgent dependency needs and one runs off, and both are left with their intense needs unsatisfied, what are they apt to do? Find other partners to hang them on, of course.

This is how a caseworker at the Family Service of Dedham wraps up the situation:

"It's musical chairs. The runaway often finds someone to move in with right away, and the spouse left behind finds someone to move in with also. Someone from another part of the country, maybe, running from another marriage. Both partners build nests for themselves.

"Someone who runs is bound to repeat old patterns no matter where they run to. They can't break them unless they do an awful lot of work on them."

It's worth returning to the example of Harvey and Joanna, described in Chapter 6, whose marriage came to an abrupt end when Joanna was about to have a baby and Harvey, who couldn't stand the idea of sharing Joanna with anyone, ran away. There is more to their story than that, and it illustrates the musical chairs principle.

For a time Joanna had no idea where Harvey went. She had the child. Tried to cope alone. Eventually, through a friend who accidentally ran into him, she learned Harvey was in Miami working in a leather goods shop. Impulsively, Joanna got on a plane and headed for Florida. She found Harvey; they spent three emotional days together. She alternated between loving and hating him. He didn't mention their child once except to offer to pay child support; Joanna instinctively knew this was just a gesture of the moment. He refused to talk about the business and financial mess he'd left behind. He told her he was alternately living with two women. "Both," he said, "are doing a very good job of taking care of me."

Joanna went back to Chicago utterly depressed. But she came home with more of a sense of reality as well. As the therapist to whom Joanna subsequently went for treatment said, "Finding her runaway husband really helped her recognize that he wasn't going to come back on a white charger and rescue her."

However, Joanna wasn't through with Harvey. She became heavily involved with another man who was highly needy and whose neediness sustained her; as with Harvey, she was dependent on his dependence. After a few months of somewhat more intensive therapy, she saw how much this man and Harvey resembled each other, and that she was tying into this man's neurotic pattern just as she had tied into Harvey's. Soon she put an end to the relationship.

Joanna's story has a happy ending. In time she found another man, but this one was kind and supportive, he could give as well as take. They married. But where is her ex-husband, runaway Harvey? As far as Joanna knows, he is as he was — a dependent.

9

Other Wanderers:
Floaters and Oldsters

Hard-Times Nomads

The word "runaways" evokes familiar images: children sneaking off at dawn, husbands pretending to go to work as usual and never returning to their waiting families, wives disappearing while their husbands and children are safely off at their jobs and schools. But anyone who is familiar with the work of Travelers Aid offices and skid row missions, or has studied the bus stations and the seamier sections of town, or listens to the stories police and social workers tell, becomes aware of the fact that the runaway phenomenon is much more complicated than that.

Whenever money is short and jobs are scarce, a segment of the rooted members of society becomes uprooted. The Depression years showed us in the most vivid and poignant way how hard times produce migrants, nomads and restless wanderers. Hordes of economically and psychologically depressed human beings roamed the dusty countrysides and infiltrated the distressed cities. They looked for something to eat. They sought work. They were grateful for handouts. But not only in the Depression years. Both before and since, the same transmutations and peregrinations have taken place. They're going on now, in this season of our economic discontent, with upward of eight percent of the American population unemployed.

Many of the present wanderers are the counterculture heroes of the last decade, the young men and women who said the hell with it all — the hell with college, with jobs, with split-level paradises and all the other trappings of American society. Whether their political stances were wholly sincere or whether their righteousness served to justify a joyful irresponsibility, the end result is the same. Many are unskilled. Many are uneducated, at least in terms of a marketable education. They lack the tools for survival at a time when survival is tough even for some of the fittest.

In a sense their time is out of joint. They cling to a past that bears little relationship to the job-hungry present and suffer the psychological wounds of dislocation. Early in 1976 *The New York Times* asked fourteen youth service specialists around the country to assess the young men and women who grew up in the sixties. The consensus: "Large numbers . . . are now experiencing a general malaise of haunting frustrations, anxiety and depression."

So it is that since 1970 or so young "floaters" have popped up in Los Angeles, in Washington, in Boston — wherever their mood takes them, wherever they fancy the possibility of some work or some fun. They consist mostly of couples in their twenties. Many are married. Many are living together in committed relationships.

Having dropped out in the sixties, they have no way of dropping into the seventies. It is more than just the fact that they lack skills that will get them decent jobs. They still have strong ambivalences about working, about leading the conventional life. They're still alienated from the prevailing values of society. What they really want to do is reenter society on their own terms, which in effect means half-entry. Some have children whom they love. Their commitment to their families is the psychic structure that sustains them in an otherwise unstructured life.

Maybe they can't properly be termed runaways. They're not running from parents (though they may have done so as adolescents). They're certainly not running from spouses. Yet they do run — from places that don't give them work, that don't provide them with the kind of life they want; they run from life-styles they find uncomfortable. There is enough to run from to keep them in perpetual motion. They've run long enough, often enough, to make running an end in itself.

Many of these young couples turn out to come from solidly working-class families, but blue-collar jobs in plants and factories and gas stations and warehouses aren't for them. Being cooped up in offices or stores would be anathema (besides, no one will hire them for such jobs). What do they want? "What we want is . . . uh . . . " By this time they often don't really know. They impart a feeling of vagueness. The image they present is fuzzy and out of focus.

A number of social workers, in discussing the young floaters, commented on their "spacey" quality. This could be due to constant moving or not eating well or drugs. Give them a slip of paper to a welfare office and they lose it. Line them up with a job and they can't seem to make the connection. Yet it is not only drugs. These vague, wandering children of eighteen and twenty and twenty-five still worship the god of spontaneity: meet a guy in a burger joint, the vibes are good, he invites you to crash at his place — that's what it's all about.

Mental Patients

Can escapees from mental institutions truly be called runaways? The fact is that they do run from their hospitals or other facilities. They do leave without official approval, these voluntary commitments (there are few of the other kind these days) — disturbed men and women who yearn for a freedom they usually can't handle. Many cannot fend for themselves. Once out they find that even the missions and skid row shelters that cater to drunks don't welcome them: what person in his right mind wants to take in crazies who may suddenly beat their heads against a wall or start howling in the middle of the night? Sometimes even the hospitals from which they ran are relieved to have them gone and make little effort to retrieve them.

So these sad and wasted human beings, some only in their early twenties, some as old as their late sixties, also become eternal wanderers. Unlike the young floaters, though, they're still looking for a home. And what about their homes of old, the families whence they came? No "welcome back" signs are put up. Their kin, their spouses, have had enough.

"When they come to our attention we try to find their families, try to get them to take them back," says Charles W. Liddell, executive director of the Travelers Aid Society of Boston. "Or, if they won't take them back, at least get them on welfare and give them whatever aid they can. But most of their relatives have long since become very tired of the whole situation. These people are at the bottom of the barrel."

Vietnam Vets on the Street

Can Vietnam veterans be left out of the runaway category? Some do flee. A few run from their parental homes; many leave their wives and children. Most are on the low end of the socioeconomic scale, most grew up imbued with the dream of making it big as men. In Vietnam they *were* men, in their terms — heroes, some of them — and whether they stormed an enemy stronghold or razed a village inhabited by women, children and old men, they did the job their superiors expected them to do.

Eventually, though, they had to return home. They came back home not to a hero's applause but to jungle traps of a different kind than those in Vietnam, but vicious traps just the same. Many of the returnees brought home a new trap — the heroin habit; many had limbs shot off or were otherwise disabled from their Asiatic adventures. For many who came from ghetto schools, soldiering was the only refined skill they had (and soldiering is definitely not listed in the employment classifieds). A fair number had married their childhood sweethearts before going over; it was a way of fortifying themselves to do their brave man's work. Some others swept their sweethearts to the altar afterward, in the first passionate flush of homecoming. It would, they hoped, give them stability and meaning here. So many of them were or became husbands and fathers and wanted to be good family men. But given the realities of life, how was it possible for them to be what they wanted to be?

Hardly possible at all, said a man who worked as a counselor with drug-addicted and runaway Vietnam vets at Phoenix House, a drug rehabilitation center in New York City. The counselor, deeply troubled by the plight of these men, went on to say, "After being used to killing they came home to America and were expected to be content to live quietly, drawing their little paychecks if they were lucky enough to get jobs. And not relate to violence. To cut all that part of them off. A lot of them love their families and want to get on with the job of taking care of their families. A family life consists of a series of loving exchanges, you know? But they had to cut off those sensitive parts of themselves in order to do what they were supposed to do in 'Nam. So there's a lot of inner turmoil and when it starts coming up to the top, and starts choking them, they take something to put it back down. When they can't get jobs and have to make it with a family, they take something. So they're shooting dope and spending more and more of their time on the streets. Then they have to do things to get the dope and they don't want their families involved, and they're ashamed, so they split — wind up in a V.A. hospital here, or just manage to survive on the streets. Yeah, they're runaways."

Once a Counterculture Girl . . .

Ought former counterculture girls who can't make it in straight society be numbered among the runaways? If the floater couples are, so should they be, though they come to their runaway status by another route. Many of these young women are college dropouts. Many are very bright. A number have dabbled in the arts. They escaped parental caring, which they saw as tyranny, to be taken care of in communal settings. But as the communes dwindled they had no hold, no one upon whom they could rely. And what does a woman easily come to rely upon, or return to for reliance, when there is nothing else? What she has from girlhood been taught to rely upon — a man. So they marry. They become wives of "straight" men who, just like Daddy, are serious about money and success. They become mothers. They're expected to raise their kids in good upstanding middle-class fashion.

But from hippie lass to model wife is not a transformation easily accomplished. For a number of these young women a few years of being an ordinary wife and mother are quite enough. They feel stifled, cornered. And some revert to old ways and drop out; some run away. While they think that leaving their families far behind is the cure they need, at best it serves as a temporary palliative. They move about as runaways, feeling guilty, angry, depressed. Thoughts of suicide creep in. They have a hard time focusing. They come across the way they look — a little fuzzy around the edges.

Sometimes the people around them think, "How well she's doing now" — and then, suddenly, off these young women go. Nancy is one. She passed through a hippie adolescence, even spending time in a commune, while her middle-class parents wrung their hands and her mother kept saying, "Nancy, what's to become of you?" Eventually she seemed to pass out of that stage. She met and married someone reassuringly solid, an architecture student. For a few years she led the conventional life and her mother beamed. Nancy's husband finished school, his career flowered, she bore him two children. They built themselves a fabulous house that he designed. "It's a dream come true," Nancy's mother said. On the day they were to move in, Nancy ran away.

When women like Nancy come to social service agencies for help, as they sometimes do, they know something is wrong with them. They know they want help for their disordered lives. But they don't have any specific notions of what it is they're after. They say something vague like, "I don't know what's the matter with me."

According to Naumi Alcalay, who has counseled a number of them, "For these young women, most in their twenties, the old life-style has ended and they question, 'What do I do now? Where do I go? What's my relationship to society, to my ideals, to my fellow man, to people with whom I'm involved?' They attempt to fight these questions with some crazy acting out, usually of a sexual nature, which is totally unsatisfying. And then they collapse in a deep depression. And usually these women leave everything and run. They don't even stay in treatment long enough to be helped, they run from it, too — going on to another state, another part of the country."

Geriatric Runaways

Who would expect to find sixty- and seventy-year-old runaways? Yet there is a contingent of geriatric runaways, elderly men and women who show up in many of the same places that draw the younger runaways. And they run for some of the same reasons.

Senior citizens are no more immune to marital unhappiness than anyone else. Nor are they necessarily calmer in the face of prospective marital dissolution. So there are men and women — mostly men — who leave their mates without warning, without the formalities. In some instances they've been married for forty years or so, and have finally had enough. They take their last Social Security checks and depart.

If they wind up in some other city, stranded and lost, they're likely to come to the attention of a social service agency. Then a telephone call to their wives made on their behalf is apt to bring the sharp reply, "I don't want him back!" Sometimes, with a little remorse on the man's part, a little time for the wife to get over her anger, a reconciliation can be effected. Sometimes not.

At the Family Location and Legal Services in New York City, another runaway-spouse pattern is sometimes seen. It involves older men — men in their seventies, say — who were fairly happily married for thirty-five or forty years. Their wives die. They are painfully lonely; they meet widows as lonely as they — women who seem nice.

Such a man thinks, "She won't replace my wife, may she rest in peace, but maybe we can find some happiness together." They marry. His dream vanishes in an endless round of bickering. Six months is enough. He can't stand to be with this woman. But how can a man his age — and he's not well, either — face the trauma of separation and divorce? Besides, maybe she's going to want him to pay alimony. He is confused. Trapped. So he runs away.

Most often men like this one run to their children. But
when they're located, says a social worker who has worked
with them, "they're happy to cooperate when approached
for a divorce. They didn't know how to go about it themselves, they were afraid it would cost them a lot of money —
and they weren't ever going to remarry so they didn't bother
about getting divorced."

There are other reasons why the aged run. For a long time
the nation's capital, *their* capital, was their magnet, just as
Haight-Ashbury drew the counterculture kids. They ran away
from home to see their senators, their congressmen, they
wanted to have a few words with the President of the United
States. A bit senile, a bit naive, hopeful, desperate and confused, they wanted to exchange words with *somebody* very
important about their plight. What with food so high, rents
impossible, they could hardly make ends meet, they wanted
to say; they wanted to explain that sometimes they had to
choose between eating and buying the medicines they needed.

With the advent of Medicaid and Medicare and supplementary Social Security payments, the number of old people
making this pathetic pilgrimage has fallen off considerably.
Now they're more apt to bring their heartbreaking stories to
officials in their home communities. But agencies like Travelers Aid Society of Washington, D.C., which used to see
them in droves, still help the relatively few who show up.

This community service agency and others like it also see
men and women who wander away from their nursing homes,
make their way to the local bus stations and, with a few
dollars hoarded over time, buy themselves transportation.
Senile and befuddled, they don't really know where they're
going. They do know that they can't bear staying in those
nursing homes.

In explaining why they ran away, they sometimes say,
"The food there is terrible." Or, "The staff is mean." Or,

"The bedding isn't changed often enough." They may not be definite about the reasons but their desperation is clear — they want to leave. Sometimes they show up in a bus station far from where they ran, wearing only bathrobes and slippers. It is what they wore when they left the institution. They'd given no thought to anything but fleeing.

Several Travelers Aid caseworkers said that they investigate an aged person's complaints — or have the T.A. office nearest the institution they ran from investigate it. They will act as the runaway's advocate, getting in touch with his or her family, possibly arranging a transfer to another rest-home facility.

Still another group of aged runaways have been discharged from mental hospitals. They're chronically ill, senile, and they can't take care of themselves. They're supposed to receive at least outpatient care in their home communities but the care often isn't available, the vital backup services don't exist. So they hit the road, they wander.

And if by chance they do come into contact with a compassionate social worker, doctor or bureaucrat willing to help, it frequently turns out that their families are no longer so compassionate. Their families, in effect, wash their hands of them.

They run from spouses, from institutions, and sometimes also from their own children, the grown children who are taking care of them. They remember — dimly, maybe, but the memory is there — how it was for them when they were younger, stronger and independent. They want so much to be independent again, for to be independent is to be young again. They want to prove to the world that they can still take care of themselves. Clutching their valises, their month's Social Security payments stuffed in a pocket, off they go.

"Then they're stranded until the first of the month," says a caseworker at the Travelers Aid Society of San Francisco.

"They aren't rooted in reality. They come to visit a friend. They have a vague idea where the friend lived. It's all on impulse."

At the Travelers Aid headquarters in Los Angeles, hard by skid row and the bus station, a senior caseworker tells the same story. Older people come to her agency from as far away as Bangor, Maine, or Miami, Florida. "Often they don't even know they're in L.A.," she explains. "They say, 'Well, I thought I would visit Aunt Jane in Kansas.' Usually they're upset about something that's been going on in their children's homes. 'The housekeeping's poor.' Or, 'My son or daughter doesn't give me the respect I deserve.'"

But there and elsewhere uglier stories, too, are sometimes heard: "My son or daughter hits me." And, "My child takes my Social Security payments and doesn't give me any money." And, "My child doesn't let me have any friends."

Sick, unwanted by their children, cantankerous, these old people have little going for them. Many of them aren't adorable Edmund Gwenn types in mentally debilitated form. We are what we are, and what we were: people when old are reflections of themselves when young — but a reflection intensified. If they were hard, querulous or otherwise unlovable throughout their lives, they've become more so in their later years. As one social worker with a large clientele of such patients remarked, "They were never able to relate well to others, and the older they become the more rigid they are. They can't fit in anywhere now."

Crisis Flight

There is another army of wanderers: perpetual ones, compulsive runners, itinerant humans whose urgent need is not to become rooted but to remain uprooted. Their itch to travel can't ever be scratched away. For them sanity lies in moving rather than in settling down.

Their category of running has been defined as "crisis flight" and these people are always in a state of crisis. All adult ages are represented, and both sexes and every socioeconomic background. They include middle-aged widows and boys of twenty and welfare couples and professional men. What they all have in common is that they can't stop being refugees. They don't really care where they're going. Their search, if it can be called that, is illusory; for them, each new destination becomes a new point of departure.

Some of these people are delusional: Art, a young man seen by caseworkers at the Travelers Aid Society of Boston, is. When he showed up, thin and bony, Art explained that he has to keep moving because if he stops the devils will catch up with him and infest his body. He eats only when he can no longer tolerate hunger; then he pushes something down his throat, dashes back to the Greyhound, and is on his way again. He has just one change of clothing. Whenever he needs money his father sends him some via Western Union. He is in perpetual flight but of no harm to anyone.

It was Catherine Hiatt of the Travelers Aid Society of Washington, D.C., who coined the term "crisis flight." She was speaking of the phenomenon at an American Orthopsychiatric Association meeting in 1969, and saw the phrase picked up by the world press to describe a new form of addiction.

"Crisis flight," she said at the time, "describes a definite pattern of travel wherein 'motionless' and geographical fleeing have become a chronically episodic way of coping — characteristic of a way of life or life style."

And now, having observed them closely all these years, Ms. Hiatt says that with these nomads neither crisis intervention nor short-term therapy really works. "It's not possible to provide them with a different structure to replace the old. Often you can send them back home for a little while, then they'll start out again."

It was a middle-aged lady from New York City who alerted Ms. Hiatt to this phenomenon. Every so often she'd use her welfare check to come to Washington to complain about the city's mayor, about New York's state senators, about other local officials — and then, having run out of funds, apply to the Travelers Aid office for financial help. Her energy seemed boundless and the agency obviously couldn't underwrite her activist shuttles indefinitely.

So her sources of funding dried up and she landed in Bellevue Hospital's psychiatric ward. Investigating further, the T.A. staff found that a number of other clients also experienced psychotic episodes if they couldn't stick to their patterns of mobility. In other words: if circumstances prevented them from keeping mobile, after some months in one spot they fell apart. Moving about gives such people a sense of balance and purpose.

Moving about can be accomplished without crossing one's geographical boundaries. "Motionless flight" includes the executive who keeps job-hopping, the professor who seeks placement with a different school each year or two, the people who must periodically replace their lovers. Motionless flight serves some persons; others are floaters who must cross geographical boundaries in order to remain sane and happy, or as sane and happy as they can be. But crossing those boundaries doesn't necessarily mean leading empty lives. Traveling salesmen, merchant seamen, truckdrivers, affluent jet-setters — all such compulsive travelers and more have found socially acceptable ways of dealing with their compulsion. They don't become a problem to themselves or others. They don't use up public and philanthropic resources. Yet there *is* a kinship between them and the floaters who have been in ten cities within fifteen months and now wind up in Boston, say, broke and disoriented.

The floaters whom social service agencies like Travelers Aid in Boston or Washington see tend to have similar kinds of backgrounds. Family instability ranks prominently. Many come from broken homes. Many grew up in a series of foster homes or one-parent families. Many experienced little or no emotional intimacy with parents or parent-substitutes when they were children. Another significant factor: as children they did a lot of moving about from place to place; their families never stayed anywhere for long.

Not everybody who grows up in a broken home or has moved about a good deal as a child is going to wind up in crisis flight, of course. But if there is a considerable amount of instability and uprootedness in the growing child's life, that child is likely to opt for mobility rather than rootedness as an approach to life.

However, incorporating rootlessness into one's psyche doesn't automatically trap one into becoming a floater. According to Ms. Hiatt, it often takes a specific life experience — a painful experience — to trigger the first crisis flight. The first crisis flight is followed by a second and third and fourth. Having to take on the responsibilities of adulthood, being fired from a job, losing a mate — such traumatic events can precipitate that first flight.

Some floaters first learned to flee in a crisis when they were adolescents. Travelers Aid offices see floaters in the making: older teenagers who have run away because they're angry with their parents, angry because they can't find decent jobs, angry because they're expected to take jobs, angry for whatever reason, wanting to get away from home — yet having no plan, no destination or goal in mind.

"Many angry young people want a bus ticket, and don't care where it's to, and don't want any questions asked, thank you very much," Ms. Hiatt said. "Particularly among the eighteen- and nineteen-year-olds you get a sense that this flight is the substitute for throwing rocks or breaking windows of the local school. It's their alternative to vandalism."

Another cluster of crisis-flighters is composed of menopausal women who have experienced a significant change in their lives — all of their children have left the nest, for instance, or they've lost their husbands through death or divorce. They may return home after a time but run again when another crisis presents itself. Or they may simply keep on going the first time. Either way, they respond to hurtful episodes in their lives by running.

A few years ago a psychiatrist, Dr. Martin Goldberg, studied over five hundred crisis-flighters who came to the Travelers Aid Society of Philadelphia for help. What he finally saw taking shape was a fairly predictable psychological profile. These people are impulsive. They're hyperactive. They're extremely dependent — though the male compulsive movers tend to mask that dependency by a show of aggressiveness or hostility. To give the impression of being active and independent, for instance, they hustle up job interviews one after the other. Yet none of those interviews ever seems to work out, because they say or do things that will ensure their being turned down.

Crisis-flighters of both sexes tend to have trouble in expressing their feelings, in getting emotionally close to people. In fact, their horror at becoming emotionally intimate with other people is one of the basic reasons they keep moving from place to place. As soon as a close relationship seems to be developing, even superficially, they feel edgy. Uncomfortable. Then they have to get out.

The more they flee, they more they need to flee: running indeed becomes an addiction. The more used to fleeing they become, the less successful mental health intervention tends to be. There are hundreds of thousands of such people out there, keeping the long-distance bus companies happy. They are unique: they *never* stop.

PART FOUR:

Coping

IO

For Parents: What To Do
When Kids Run—
Or Threaten To

"I Wonder How Well They Know Their Own Kids"

What is the one best time to deal with an adolescent's
runaway episode? Obviously, before it ever begins. Happy —
even mildly happy — teenagers don't usually split from home
(except for the occasional boy or girl who skips off briefly
on a lark). Most adolescents run because they feel compelled
to; whatever pressures they're under have become impossible
to handle. This holds as true for the youth who needs a
couple of days away from home to cool off as it does for the
one whose home life is unbearable. The difference between
them is one of degree.

Despite the mythology around him, even Huckleberry
Finn, the most celebrated runaway of American folklore,
didn't run for the fun of it. His father was a drunkard who
cursed him, beat him, tried to steal his money and made

him work in slavelike fashion under the threat of more beatings.

That teenagers run away because they're so miserable — and, often, miserable at home — is hard for most of their parents to accept. It is easier to cast blame than to acknowledge that somehow they're involved in the problem. Runaway-house counselors see this repeatedly as mothers and fathers arrive for their first meeting with their children following the runaway episode. The parents immediately slip into a blaming and accusing stance: *My kid doesn't obey the rules; my kid won't listen to anything I say; my kid promises to come home by twelve, promises to do his homework, promises to stop smoking dope — and never keeps his promises.*

Too, there is only one issue many parents want to deal with at first — the fact that the kid ran away. "Wasn't that a terrible thing he did?" They don't deliberately plan to dodge their own possible involvement in the situation, but that's how it works out.

More than a few parents are genuinely puzzled, as well as genuinely distressed, by what has happened. "But why? I don't understand!" Yet it is clear that boys and girls don't suddenly take off; as has already been discussed, they signal their troubled state for some time beforehand. They may not come right out and say what is wrong — they definitely won't if they feel they aren't being listened to. But by doing badly in school, withdrawing from peers, becoming rude and sullen at home, breaking the rules, turning heavily to drugs and other such "acting-out" behaviors they send the crucial message.

When there has been a sudden change in the family structure, such as separation, divorce or death, those warning signals may come on with startling abruptness; otherwise they probably have been showing themselves for some time.

"When the family situation is fairly stable and parents

talk about a sudden change I wonder about their perception of reality — I wonder how well they know their own kids," observes Seabury Barn's Carol Tweedy.

A close look usually shows that, though such a family has been experiencing serious conflicts for a long time, its members have been carrying on as if they were the happy Waltons. If the troubled child's troubling behavior is serious and sustained enough to catch parental attention, the parents involved are apt to use denial to minimize the seriousness of the situation. The mother of a San Diego girl who flunked classes, popped pills, got caught shoplifting and committing vandalism, and then ran away, recalls how she and her husband reacted until the girl took off: "We kept saying it was an early adolescent phase. She kept breaking rules and doing way-out things, and we kept telling ourselves that soon it would pass. We kept wanting to believe things weren't as serious as they really were."

This mother and father were doing some "magical thinking," hoping that the girl's distressing behavior would disappear if they refused to pay attention to it. They were denying the painful reality that her conduct was symptomatic of just how disturbed she really was. In the long run denial is very damaging to everybody concerned.

Family Issues

A runaway is created not because there are parent-related or other problems in a child's life — every child has problems — but because too much time elapses before they're dealt with. Soon after signs of disturbance first manifest themselves, not when the child involved runs amok, is the best time for parents to look closely at what is going on.

Of course, boys and girls don't run away only because of home-based conflicts. Other unhappy events — say, in their school or social lives — may be the trigger. Even so, the parent-child relationship may be — and probably is — a factor. Alice left home after she and her boyfriend broke up and her father refused to take her unhappiness seriously. Bill took off after he and his English teacher had an argument and the teacher promised to flunk him; Bill couldn't bear to face his parents. Vivian ran after discovering she was pregnant; she, too, was afraid and ashamed to confront her parents with the news.

Question: When *do* kids come home with bad news of one kind or another?

Answer: When they and their parents are used to talking frankly about sensitive issues.

When they don't expect their parents to be harsh and judgmental about the problem at hand, whether it's poor grades or pregnancy.

When they feel they can count on their parents' understanding.

When their parents haven't made them scapegoats by being unfairly strict and accusatory because of their own insecurities, or by picking on them to avoid dealing with a troubled marriage.

When they trust their parents.

"What's missing in the parent-child relationship tends to get played out in lack of trust and in the 'rules syndrome,'" says social worker Ron Johnson of the Family and Children's Service of Minneapolis. "Both the parents and the kids cooperate in this — cooperate in dealing with certain emotional issues on another, easier level. Parents say, 'I've been strict, I've loosened up, no matter what I do, it's not enough.' So, even though they may agree on certain rules and liberties, very soon the agreement wanes — because that's not where the real problem is."

Where does the real problem lie? More to the point, how do parents who no longer want to duck their children's troubled state get at the root of things?

Not easily. Often, in fact, it is just too much to ask family members caught up in unconscious but destructive patterns of relating to uncover, isolate and discard these patterns by themselves. This is a situation in which an objective outsider may offer the best kind of help. Sometimes families can turn (with profit) to an insightful and impartial relative or family friend — someone who's trusted and accepted by everybody involved.

On the other hand, a skilled professional associated with a child guidance center or a family service agency may be the best bet. Some runaway houses now offer preventive counseling with parents and teenagers. (See Where to Get Help.) At Valley Youth House in Bethlehem, Pennsylvania, for example, parents are welcome to come in for a session related to a troubled teenager. The teenager is also welcome to seek help or to join them for counseling. But there, as at other runaway houses that offer such services, every effort is made to ensure that the adolescent is coming in of his own free will. Coercion is antithetical to runaway-house philosophy.

Another source parents might fruitfully explore when their children are behaving in disturbed and disturbing fashion is Families Anonymous (F.A.). There are chapters in forty-two cities and more are being formed by distressed mothers and fathers.

A self-help group patterned after Alcoholics Anonymous and Al-Anon, F.A. was first started in the Los Angeles area by a handful of parents of drug-addicted children. Now, however, not only parents whose adolescents and pre-adolescents are taking drugs, but also those whose children steal, commit serious acts of vandalism, are sexually promiscuous, run away from home and in other extreme ways show their unhappiness are drawn to the weekly meetings.

These get-togethers aren't instructional in the sense that participants are told the best ways to raise their children. What parents do get are the insights, the shared experiences, of other parents who have been through it all and the sense that, whatever they're going through, they're not alone; their problems may not even be as severe as those of some others in the group. When one is bogged down with worry and anxiety about one's own child, such a discovery can be wonderfully heartening. And — maybe most important of all — participants gain the sympathy, understanding and strength that come from group support.

"I'm Going to Run Away"

Some teenagers don't stop with warning signs. They come right out with it: "If you don't give me this — if you don't let me do that — I'm going to run away!"

The easiest and most oft-adopted parental response is to go to extremes. One extreme is to establish who's in charge. The parent shouts, "Then go ahead!" This both says, "I won't let you challenge my parental authority," and, "I won't let you manipulate me into anything."

The approach tends to be counterproductive. To tell an incipient runaway, "Go ahead and run!" is like telling a potential suicide perched on a ledge to jump. It may just work — but chances are good that this will be the final push over the edge. The teenager hears the dare. He thinks, "They don't love me and want me to go," or thinks, "The bastards are challenging me — I'll show 'em!" The teenager's most likely response is to storm out the door — and whether he'll be gone a couple of hours, a couple of days or a couple of months is anybody's guess.

Another scenario:

CHILD: I'm going to run away!

PARENT: Then go!

CHILD (heading out the door): Okay!

PARENT (blocking his path): Wait, I didn't mean it!

The child may not run, but the stage has been set for repeat performances. He knows that his threat is potent, that the parent will back down. He has learned how to push another button and watch the parent jump.

Still another scenario:

CHILD: I'm going to run away!

PARENT: Well, if you must, you must; I can't stop you.

What this parent is really engaging in is "passive acceptance," but what comes across to the child is another form of quiet encouragement to go. The parent may be a fatalist, but to the kid his words have the ring of dismissal and rejection. This is hardly heartening to a child who already feels unloved, or feels that his particular place in the family structure is tentative at best.

Then there's the outright prohibition:

CHILD: I'm going to run away!

PARENT (angrily): No, you can't! I won't let you!

The futility of saying no should be self-evident. If the teenager intends to run, no power on earth can stop him. He may not run off that very moment, but he can sneak out in the middle of the night, the next day, any time. The parent can shout, "No!" as often as he cares to. The child has won.

What, then, is the right way to handle a threat to run? By listening with one's "third ear," by listening for the message behind the words, by getting (at least trying to get) at what is *behind* the threat to run. Communication. If it works, it can even end up bringing a family closer together.

When threatening to take off, a teenager may be saying, "I need your help." Or, "I need some space for myself, need to be away right now." Or, "There's some pressure on me I've got to escape from just now." Or, "I can't get anywhere with you, you don't listen."

Now it is up to that teenager's mother and father to try to explore what is actually going on. Gently. Patiently. A demand to know is just another pressure. A concerned request, a kind plea, is not.

Depending on the situation, "cooperation" may involve

letting up on the youth with respect to a subject that is sensitive just then. It may mean suggesting, "Why not take a walk and cool off?" It may mean saying, "It's all right to skip going to school for a day or two." It may mean helping the teenager arrange a weekend vacation with out-of-town friends or relatives. All of these approaches have been used successfully by parents in appropriate situations. Sometimes a protracted stay elsewhere, if it can be arranged, is a good idea. There are sets of friendly parents who, with the consent of everybody concerned, have worked out exchanges. Distressed children do better with other people's parents at times — and the parents do better, too — than with their own.

Whatever the specifics, the very fact that the incipient runaway's parents are willing to cooperate is important. It conveys love, respect and nonjudgmental concern.

Just because parents say they want to cooperate doesn't mean the troubled adolescent is going to open up. What then? Then it might be helpful to shift the talk calmly to the practical aspects of running away:

"Have you given any thought to where you would go?"

"How would you live?"

"What do you hope to accomplish by running away?"

"Why do you think running's better than staying home?"

The answers to such questions could be very revealing; what's more, a cool but concerned approach may do much to defuse the explosive situation. But it doesn't suffice to ask questions and listen carefully to the answers. Youth counselors suggest that parents who are genuinely concerned, and who really don't want their children to run away, tell them exactly that: "I love you, I hope you won't run away."

That may seem obvious, even tepid. But it conveys two very important things: that the teenager's parents do care about him and, just as significant, that he has a choice in the conduct of his life.

When a Child Runs — Emotional Turmoil

Even with the best of intentions and the most effective textbook approaches it is not always possible to forestall a runaway episode. The parents involved have two factors to deal with as soon as their child has run away: what to do about it concretely, and how to handle the event emotionally.

If this is the first or second time the child has run away — repeat performances tend to dull the agony — they're likely to be gripped by anger, guilt and intense feelings of inadequacy. "I tore myself apart," recalls the mother of the San Diego girl who took drugs and shoplifted and vandalized before running away. "I flagellated myself with all kinds of accusations. Why didn't I stay home while Ann was growing up, instead of being a working mother? Why didn't I give her ballet lessons when she was five? Why did I say no when the job of being her Girl Scout leader was offered to me? It went on and on — all those whys."

Beyond feelings of anger and guilt and inadequacy is tremendous worry and concern: *Where is my child? What's happening to my child?* Terrible fantasies spring to life (especially if the runaway is a girl). Parents think about rape, drugs, violence; about their children starving, their children molested, their children huddled in filthy alleys or rooms.

Beyond horrible visions, even, are the profound feelings of having been abandoned and deserted by one's children. Only suicide is a more blatant and painful form of rejection.

Of all those feelings anger may actually be the most difficult for parents to accept and deal with. Even in this era, openly expressed anger is still somewhat of a taboo in our society. Then, too, how can one feel angry when one's child may be sick or hurt somewhere? How can one feel angry when one feels so self-accusatory?

Yet, contradictory as it may seem, anger is a perfectly normal and natural response under the circumstances. Whether it is a child running away, a spouse becoming seriously ill, someone beloved dying, one irrational but inevitable reaction is, "How can he do that to me?"

When feelings of whatever kind are coursing through one's psyche, they demand to be accepted and expressed. They can either be accepted and expressed directly or repressed and allowed to come out only circuitously and destructively. One destructive effect of not accepting negative feelings like anger is that these feelings are intensified: "I feel angry; I feel guilty about feeling angry; I feel even more angry because I'm feeling guilty." Another destructive effect is that the anger is unloaded all at once in an avalanche of passion when the parents have their first post-runaway confrontation with their children.

Parents of runaway children also do themselves a great service when they avoid, as much as they possibly can, "projecting" about the runaway's plight. To "project" in this context is to make assumptions based on incomplete data. Mothers and fathers who know nothing of their child's immediate circumstances can drive themselves wild or sick projecting all kinds of dire events. This only serves to heighten their feelings of guilt and anger, to make them more panicky, when they really have nothing factual to go on.

Don Thibeau, a staff member at SAJA Runaway House in Washington, D.C., observes: "The daughter will run away, and the parents immediately assume she's run to California, is living a promiscuous life and taking all kinds of drugs — when the kid is actually down the street, scared stiff, lonely, maybe living with a friend. And when they find out, the parents will be so angry at the young person for having worried them so, they may never get over it."

In sorting out their own feelings and deciding what course of action to take, it is helpful for the parents to give thought to what their runaway is feeling. Youths who run also harbor a gamut of conflicting emotions. There's the thrill, the excitement, of running. Then there's the anger against their parents. They have tons of it. Just as mothers and fathers tend to overstate the calamity of the situation, so do the kids tend to overstate their parents' culpability. *J'accuse* — so many accusations, so many parental shortcomings to rage about, their heads are filled with justifications for running. They externalize everything; they can't — at least in this emotion-laden time — see their own role in the events that have come to pass.

Just as parents find it hard to acknowledge their anger, so do the runaways find it hard to accept their own guilty feelings. But guilt is there, underneath, in ample measure. And fear, as well: their parents wonder anxiously about what's happening to them "out there"; they wonder anxiously about themselves "out there."

And, even though they pretend they don't care a bit, they do wonder what their parents are thinking, feeling, doing about their having run away. They're not in the mood to give their folks the benefit of the doubt, yet want proof that they're wanted at home, after all. They're very likely to put their parents in a "no-win" position. Calling in the police is a case in point. The child whose parents do call the police is apt to snarl, "You even turned me in to the cops!" When parents don't file a report, the child is liable to wail, "You don't even care enough to report me missing!"

Police Work — Pros and Cons

Should the police be notified? If so, how soon? What are the advantages? The drawbacks? Are there constructive alternatives?

What happened in the case of Wanda, a fourteen-year-old
Manhattan girl, is instructive. One evening Wanda left word
on her mother's telephone answering device: "I'm spending
the night with Shirley." Because Wanda had been acting
strangely and unpleasantly since her parents' separation,
Wanda's mother phoned Shirley's mother to make sure
Wanda was indeed there. She was not. Understandably
concerned, Wanda's mother immediately began a systematic
check of all of the girls and boys listed in Wanda's address
book. Finally, at about eleven-thirty that night, she reached
one of her daughter's boyfriends. He knew where Wanda
was, but wouldn't tell, except to say that she was fine.

Because of the boy's assurances, Wanda's mother didn't
call the police. In the morning she conferred with her husband; they decided to hold off on the police for a few days.
They didn't want to alienate their distraught child further,
and they didn't want to put off her friends, who were their
only link to her. It proved the right decision. Wanda showed
up before the day was over.

As Dr. W. B. Beaser, author of *The Legal Status of Runaway Children,* points out, it is extremely difficult to make
any definitive statement about whether or not to call in the
police. There are so many variables — the age of the child,
whether this is a repeat runaway episode, whether the child
is in danger, and more. There's a greater urgency, obviously,
when a susceptible thirteen-year-old takes off than when an
experienced fifteen-year-old does.

In most instances the conservative approach is probably
the best one. Parents should first satisfy themselves that
their child has actually run away. Methodically going down
the list of the runaway's friends, also speaking to their
parents, is a very good idea. Word may get back to the
missing child that her parents are very concerned and taking
action. The runaway's friends, who may be sheltering or
otherwise protecting her, are alerted to their worry and to

the fact that the parents are searching. As in Wanda's case, one may have some news. In any event, most police departments require parents to wait forty-eight hours before filing missing persons reports, because many young runaways return by then.

There are factors besides prematurity to consider in deciding whether or not to call in the police. All police departments require the filing of a missing persons report. Some police departments won't act unless the parents involved also sign a warrant allowing officers to detain the runaway. Detention may mean a court hearing, may require the intervention of a lawyer.

In many jurisdictions if a child is from another part of the country the police department or the juvenile court contacts his parents and asks them to send plane fare so he can be shipped back home. Where he stays while waiting depends on the locality. In Las Vegas, for instance, it may be the police station or a local runaway house. In some other places — for example, in much of Utah — it may be a detention home. Many detention homes around the country are little better than jails.

Much depends on the locality, on whether the runaway has committed other offenses, on how the policemen or the juvenile court judge feel about teenage runaways. Some are humane, some are spiteful, some want to be kind but are inundated with work and don't have the time, some don't care what happens to the runaway. A warrant does increase the risk that if the runaway is picked up he'll be caught up in the cogs of the juvenile justice system.

Parents who are convinced their child is in a potentially dangerous situation have no choice about notifying the police, however. As for hearings, they need not be formal. When only a runaway episode is involved, many peace officers and judges handle the case very informally and speedily.

Some parents, fed up with their troublesome teenagers,

become hard-liners; their attitude is to "let their child go through the court process and spend a few days in a detention home." Their hope is that the child's experiences at the hands of the law will prevent future attempts at running away.

Maybe it will, maybe it won't. How it goes depends on how anxious the runaway becomes, on the level of hostility between him and his parents, on his attitude toward police and other authority figures, on his personal experiences while held in the juvenile justice system. Some teenagers are so shocked by it all that they do make an effort to face their problems, to change (but are very apt to run again if their parents aren't willing to make the same effort to face the problems). On the other hand, many youths become so angry and resentful there's no reaching them. In sum, it is a calculated risk at best.

There are parents who believe that all they have to do is file a police report and their runaways will magically be found. But in the real world no such magic occurs. Filing a missing persons report may result in an all points bulletin and nothing more. If no concrete leads to the missing teenager's whereabouts exist, there is little the police will do. No police department has the time, manpower, or inclination to track down all the youths for whom missing persons reports are filed.

What happens when such a report is filed? Boston's procedure is a fairly typical example. The parents of a runaway are asked to file a missing persons report in their local precinct. The police department then issues a bulletin, by radio, that goes to police stations all over the city. Then the information is fed into the Boston police computer. The department's missing persons bureau is very proud of its computer, which, unfortunately, merely stores all those reports that anxious parents file. (A number of big-city police departments are computer-linked to each other.)

Except in unusual cases, Boston policemen will not go out looking for the runaway if no solid leads are available. They won't assign a detective to start an investigation or develop leads. They can't — not when their priority is, or should be, the investigation of major crimes. But the Boston police and most other police departments will check out any really substantial leads that parents may have. Also, when a missing persons report is on file, it facilitates identifying the teenager as a runaway if he is coincidentally picked up on a related charge or if a police department in another city is making inquiries about him.

There is a legal mechanism known as the Interstate Juvenile Compact available to parents who want their runaway child, one who's living in another state, returned to them. The parents must know where the child is residing. They go to juvenile court and file a petition. Then the court issues a custody order. The order is sent to the appropriate state, the youth is picked up by the police, a court hearing follows. The judge decides whether to send the youth home or to a court in the runaway's home area or to a foster home. Nearly all states are members of the Compact.

Where Else to Turn

Informing the police department is one thing. Informing the rest of the world is another. Acting out of shame, guilt and embarrassment, many parents try to hide, as long as possible, the fact that their children have run away. They won't tell friends, relatives or neighbors. Both psychologically and practically, however, such secretiveness is usually a mistake. Psychologically because the anguished parents are isolating themselves from the emotional support they'd otherwise get. Practically because, by remaining silent, they're depriving themselves of potentially important sources of help. Neighbors sometimes hear things. Relatives may be able to suggest possible hiding places unknown to the parents. Friends, especially those with teenagers of their own, might well be able to offer concrete suggestions. Contacting the runaway's friends, and the friends' parents, too, is essential. Even if they really know nothing at first, the runaway may get in touch with them later on. It is a good idea, therefore, to recheck with them periodically. The runaway's teachers should also be informed; an occasional youth gets in touch with a favorite teacher or actually continues going to school while away from home.

How about employing a private detective to locate the missing adolescent? Chapter 12 deals extensively with that issue. In general detectives are expensive and their chances of success are problematical. They talk to the runaway's friends and to the other people the runaway teenager has had contact with in the daily run of life; this parents can do. Some investigators print fliers that carry the runaway's photograph and description, and offer a reward; mailings go out to police departments, runaway houses and other likely spots. This, too, is something parents can do.

Parents of runaways might do well to invest in the *National Directory of Runaway Programs,* published by the National Youth Alternatives Project. It lists most of the runaway houses in operation, the facilities they have to offer, and their principal contact persons. Generally, shelters are cooperative in pinning fliers and notes from parents on their bulletin boards.

Runaway hot lines are another resource for parents. There exist two toll-free runaway hot lines, both national in scope. Volunteer operators relay messages from teenagers who want to contact their parents but don't want to call directly. Replies from parents are then relayed to the teenagers who want them. Parents may also call the hot lines on their own to see if their missing children have left some word for them. The hot lines also act as referral agencies for teenagers who need legal, medical or psychiatric help, or who want to know where they can bed down for free. What the hot lines definitely will not do is to trace teenagers' calls for parents, or reveal in which shelter facilities the runaways are staying.

Searching on One's Own

Because most teenage runaways stick close to home these days, their parents might consider making a personal search for them. Obvious places to begin are the teenagers' hangouts — the pizza parlors, hamburger joints, parks and shopping malls they used to frequent. Private detectives suggest going to these places at different times of the day and different days of the week. They also advise speaking to the employees and managers; somebody may have seen the missing youth. In fact, the runaway may have taken a job in one or another of the shops. When parents make the rounds they should have with them recent photos of their missing children to show around.

Is there a section of town where street kids and runaways hang out? Are there urban communes in the area? Are there houses or apartments where young people are known to live communally? If so, these are also possibly fruitful areas to explore. But take care: most neighborhoods where street kids and urban communes locate are likely to be seedy or worse.

Don't count on street kids and commune dwellers, with their strong antiestablishment attitudes, to be very friendly to parents looking for their runaway children. Yet there might be sympathetic neighbors in the area willing to be of help. When rebellious sixteen-year-old Peggy vanished from her home in Torrance, California, her parents filed a police report, but otherwise did nothing. Peggy's grandmother, a woman in her mid-sixties, got into her car, drove to a borderline ghetto area where some young adults were known to be living communally and combed the neighborhood.

Going from door to door, her granddaughter's photograph in hand, she asked people if they'd seen the girl. One woman claimed to have seen her coming out of a nearby house. That night Peggy's parents went to the house but found only a scruffy-looking young woman and her little boy at home. She denied ever having seen their daughter, but seemed very nervous. Peggy's parents threatened to have everybody who lived there arrested if Peggy wasn't home by midnight. By ten of twelve a furious Peggy returned to her own house. She hadn't wanted anything to happen to the new friends who had been sheltering her.

Coercion — A Double-edged Sword

The point of Peggy's story is that parents can sometimes find their runaway kids on their own — *not* that the tactic Peggy's parents chose was necessarily effective. Teenagers may be coerced into returning home, as Peggy was, but once they're home what do you do with them? As it happened, Peggy's parents gave her the choice of continuing to stay at home but obeying rules of conduct they'd mutually arrived at, or going to live with relatives elsewhere. She chose the relatives, which dismayed her mother and father at first but turned out to be best for everybody concerned.

Coercion of the kind Peggy's parents used always carries the implication that parents consider their child as property. Their subsequent flexibility — their willingness to allow her to make a major decision in regard to her life — blunted its impact on Peggy. When a teenager is found to be in a hazardous setting, however, and is not willing to leave, the parents may have no choice but to use coercion. And the teenager may come to see that that coercion was an expression of caring, of love.

Nevertheless, coercion is usually counterproductive. It enrages and humiliates the children involved, increasing the provocation to run away again. This is demonstrated at times when runaway houses notify parents that their missing children have turned up there. Some parents are unwilling to let them stay. They're so furious they shout into the phone, "If you don't send my kid home at once I'll get the cops after you!" They may order their runaways home immediately. They may show up unannounced to bring them back or talk local police officers into picking them up. Dismayed by such reactions, shelter counselors usually give runaway youths an option when they can: to stay or leave quickly, before their parents arrive. More than one runaway has sneaked out the back door of a runaway house, belongings in hand, while his parents or the police are coming in the front door. And more than one runaway house has been the scene of an ugly confrontation as the parents or the cops corner their young quarry before she or he has had a chance to leave.

In such instances the parents may get the body back — but, youth workers correctly ask, to what end? And for how long? There is an alternative to coercion once the runaway has been located. That alternative is to try to establish communication with him, *without* forcibly returning him home — to try, through a process of careful, patient dialogue, to negotiate the return home.

The First Phone Call

Whether it emanates from a runaway house or elsewhere, whether it takes place days, weeks or months after a teenager has left, that first phone call is a very sensitive one. Often neither the teenagers, who may just want to hear their parents' voices, nor the parents themselves know what to say.

"I was so happy to hear his voice, to know he was okay,"

recalls the father of a Boston teenager who was gone three weeks before he contacted his home. "But I just didn't know what words to use, I was afraid anything I said might scare him off."

This is how many parents react — with fear as well as with joy. There is that wonderful surge of relief: "My child is alive — and sounds well!" But then comes the anxiety: *how do I keep him talking?*

Some parents go from relief and anxiety to a surge of anger over which they seem to have no control. In their recriminations, their message is a sharply guilt-producing one: "We worried ourselves sick; how could you do this to us?" And that message may be followed by an equally sharp demand: "Come home at once."

"If the child is gone, trying to force him back is not the answer," counsels Sister Barbara of Boston's The Bridge. "If the phone call is the only contact, there's a string there, the kid is still hanging on to the family. Use that in a positive way."

She and other counselors who work with runaway teenagers make these suggestions: don't put pressure on the runaway. Don't try to make him feel guilty. Because *all* teenagers want to feel they're being cared for and protected — even while they're intent on pushing for all the independence they can get — seek positive reasons why the child should come home. Tell the runaway what you're feeling — that you're happy to hear from him, that you miss him, that you love him, that you've been worried about him, that his call is very important to you, that you wish he'd come home, that you're trying to understand why he ran.

Conveying thoughts such as these may not instantly bring the teenager back; nonetheless, they're an important first step in the process of return. What is more, these may be feelings that never were clearly expressed in the parent-child relationship; in that case, the first phone call can also serve as a breakthrough in the expression of loving emotions.

Says Carol Tweedy, "All those gushy things that make people vulnerable but that essentially tie them together are the things that don't get said."

That first phone call from the runaway provides an excellent means for saying them.

Reunion

It may take several phone conversations before the runaway decides to return home, but, unless he chooses not to return at all — unlikely in the case of most teenagers — a reunion follows. Whether the runaway comes directly home or the reunion takes place under "third-party" auspices, as at a runaway house, the first meeting is as sensitive as the first phone call.

That initial get-together is apt to be explosive. Both sides — an accurate description in that they're still adversaries — face each other. Both sides are experiencing similar feelings of worry, anger and anxiety. Typically, the parents at once blame the teenager for everything that has gone wrong. Typically, the teenager is just as intent on blaming his parents. The parents provoke. The teenager provokes. Nobody listens. Typically, again, the word *trust* gets paddled about like a Ping-Pong ball.

The teenager says, "You never trust me."

The parents say, "When we start to trust you, you let us down."

The teenager replies, "If you don't trust me, the hell with you!"

The parents say, "See, we're right, we can't trust you."

Everybody feels righteously outraged, but this is a game nobody wins because it is a game without end. Each person hangs on to it grimly. Why? Because it is familiar. Who wants to be the first to try something new even if it's possibly more constructive? Who wants to take the chance? Who wants to be so vulnerable? A competent counselor, seeing the game played on and on, will try to unearth the more serious family problems that underlie the relatively superficial disagreements. He will try to get everybody involved — mother, father and the runaway — to see what each is *individually* doing to perpetuate difficulties. And he will help them develop new, more effective modes of relating to each other.

Of course, he can only do that if everybody concerned is willing to cooperate. Though many parents refuse, some counselors say that on the whole parents are more cooperative about involving themselves in family counseling than they were a few years ago. So are the runaways.

According to youth worker Cheryl Steinbuch of The Door in Manhattan, "Many times they come in thinking their parents are villains. After a time they become more aware of themselves and their own input into the situation. Then the attitude is more likely to become, 'My old man's an SOB, but there are times when I've been a stinker, too.'"

Constructive changes can't and don't occur as a result of just one counseling session. Often substantive issues aren't even dealt with at that first explosive meeting. They can't be when the parents and their child are barely talking and hardly listening to each other. Sometimes things become so tense the runaway slams out of the room. Only when the atmosphere is somewhat calmer can serious issues be grappled with. Even then, many runaway houses can only begin to help the parties concerned to deal with them, since they may not be equipped to do long-term counseling and certainly can't help those families living a considerable distance away.

All runaway houses make referrals to appropriate counseling agencies in the families' home communities, if they are available, which frequently they're not. Unfortunately, too, estimates are that three-fourths of the families on whose behalf referrals are made don't follow through. Once they're home, and with things peaceful for a few days, both the parents and the returned runaway lose their initial interest in seeking professional counseling. Then members of the family go back to the familiar old destructive ways. The familiar old problems surface. The setting is created for another runaway episode.

The emotions that froth up at the first reunion tend to be about the same whether that reunion takes place in a runaway house or at home. At home, because there is no third party in the form of a counselor to make full expression safe, both the parents and the runaway may initially be more circumspect about revealing their angry feelings too directly or sharply. Reunions are apt to be more tearful than at runaway houses.

For a few days, all are on their best behavior. Talk about problems and conflicts is carefully skirted; wishful thinking is in the air. Sooner or later, however, the pent-up hurt and angry feelings surface. There is no escaping them.

There is no escaping them, but this crisis situation can also serve as a vehicle for change — change that enables these parents and this runaway to treat each other more satisfyingly than before. In this respect the early days of a runaway's return are crucial.

Very often, in the initial stages of a return, the parents like to concentrate on the runaway episode. That episode *is* uppermost in their minds, of course. But by focusing on it they also keep themselves on the outside. They become spectators, as it were, rather than participants in a family drama that resulted in their child's running. It is less threatening for parents to see the runaway as a "problem child" than to question themselves and their own actions too closely. But it also keeps them from dealing constructively with the problems that need to be dealt with.

What, instead, is the most helpful and realistic way of looking at the situation? That no one family member is to blame. According to Andi Stromberg, of Jewish Family

Service's West Side Crisis Unit in Manhattan, "The first principle is that the 'identified patient' is not the kid who ran away. The act of running is an indication that there's trouble within the entire family, therefore the family itself becomes the patient."

Once individual family members grasp this, they can avoid continuing the self-defeating patterns of the past.

An enticing trap that many families fall into, and must avoid, is to be determinedly cheerful, effusively affectionate when the runaway returns home. Things may be fine at first. They won't be fine for long, though, because the atmosphere is forced and can't last. What it derives from is the very human wish to avoid conflicts. But the conflicts are there, lurking beneath the surface, and wishing them away won't make them go away.

In talking over the runaway episode, avoid accusations — *you did this, you did that*. Instead, express the strong feelings that you, the parent, have: "I was so worried when you called but didn't say where you were," or, "I was really angry that you took my watch to pay for the bus ticket." This approach conveys both love and limit-setting. Yes, you care; no, you definitely will not countenance breaches of decent behavior. As Stephen Torkelson of Covenant House puts it, "Kids must realize they have choices and are responsible for their own choices."

The runaway is apt to be bursting with criticism of his parents. Most of those criticisms will be hard to take; many are apt to be exaggerations of fact. But do try to listen for the truths they contain, rather than playing it easy by rejecting them all out of hand. A certain amount of self-criticism on everybody's part (who's perfect?), without being self-abasing about it, is of great help. It helps to prevent a hardening of positions that leads all the participants to behave as they did before the runaway episode took place.

Warding off a Repeat Episode

The young person ran away, the young person may run, or quite likely threaten to run, away again. Some repeaters take off two or three times, others run for as many as a dozen times or more. Repetitions are generally triggered because the first one didn't effect any of the major changes the runaway hoped for. Repetitions indicate that family members are doing to each other what they always have done, with just one thing different — the act or threat of running has itself become incorporated into the family drama.

What do a teenager's threats to run again actually mean? They obviously mean that the underlying problems have not been resolved. They also mean the runaway is trying to gain an upper hand — trying to control his parents — by the use of such threats.

That leaves it up to the parents. If they feel that henceforth they will have to tread softly in their life with the former runaway lest he take off again, then he has indeed gained control. In gaining control he also feels let down yet again, because no teenager *really* wants to be without limits. All children want to feel that their parents care enough to keep their behavior from going too far out of bounds.

Ignoring the runaway's new threats also isn't helpful, because then the parents are simply ignoring the fact that serious problems still exist. Sister Barbara suggests saying something on the order of, "We don't want you to run again, but we can't be afraid to correct you or to say no to you when necessary." Parents must stand by any such statement as this. The child must understand his parents *will* stand by it.

Can families really effect significant change without outside intervention? Often that is very difficult, if not impossible. Often the behaviors that cause so much trouble for everyone are too deeply ingrained to be located and eliminated easily. Some runaway counselors are convinced that every runaway episode that lasts for more than a day or two should be followed up by at least a consultation with a mental health professional. Family service agencies and child guidance centers, as well as psychiatrists and psychologists who work with adolescents, are counseling a growing number of families with runaway children.

Not infrequently, longer term family therapy is needed. Some mothers and fathers reject such intervention outright. They forget they have a teenager on their hands whom they have not successfully kept in the family. Therapy may not work miracles, and sometimes it doesn't work at all. But it can be a family's best chance of getting a runaway to stay home.

II

What to Do
When Your Mate Runs—
Or Returns

Families in Crisis

Ted, a middle-level executive, reacted as if shellshocked when his wife, Edna, took off without warning. Here was the woman who ran the household, mothered their two children of grammar-school age, did her chores as cook, maid, counselor, errand girl, message relayer, laundress, chauffeur and (occasional) sex partner — here was this indispensable helpmeet suddenly withdrawing her services. Gone.

Ted was used to giving orders and making decisions, especially in his work life. But in the days immediately following Edna's desertion he became a model of indecisiveness. He even seemed unable to remember some of his domestic skills. Cooking was an example. He'd cooked for himself as a bachelor and sometimes prepared a meal when Edna was tired or visiting her out-of-town sister. It hadn't been a problem. Now he found it difficult to pour breakfast cereal into bowls for the children each morning, now he hardly seemed able to shove frozen dinners into the oven.

Ted's two little girls, when they weren't asking where their mother was, had to keep reminding him to feed the family pooch. They were obviously shattered by their mother's abrupt disappearance, whispering a lot between themselves and bursting into tears when Ted became impatient with them. He was often impatient. And he was a study in anxiety.

Getting up mornings after yet another sleepless night, Ted kept finding it hard to believe that *she* had left *him*. It all seemed unbelievable, utterly unreal. If he'd answered honestly when asked how he felt in those early days, he would have had to say he felt like a little boy — an abandoned kid, one whose parents had tossed him out on the street. Finally, he put in a hurry-up call to his mother, who lived thirty miles away, to come and run the household while he figured out what to do next.

When Madge's husband, Pete, ran away, leaving her with four children to care for alone, her reaction was also one of total and complete inadequacy. Her first thought, in fact, was, "We're going to starve!" Her second thought was, "That rotten son of a bitch, how could he have done this to me?" Her third thought was, "What will my friends and relatives say?" Her fourth thought was, "Those poor kids, what am I going to tell them when they ask where their father is?"

In the days following Pete's desertion, Madge found herself doing what she later described as "crazy things." Twice she went to his place of work, an electronics supermarket where he was second-in-command in the shipping department. Ignoring the obvious fact that his disappearance had thrown the place into confusion, she screamed at everyone she saw that they were hiding Pete, or keeping his whereabouts a secret from her. With the children she became irritable, sometimes impossible. Especially so with the boys. Traditionally easygoing, she yelled at them for the slightest mischief. Because of their father's disappearance, and because of the way their mother was acting, the whinier of the children became even more whiny, and the others more mischievous.

Like Ted, Madge tossed and turned night after anguished night. Mornings she looked at herself in the mirror and thought, "God, how awful, no wonder he left, what man in his right mind would want you?" She dragged herself around; a heavy fatigue weighed her down and she spent much time just moping around the house. She was exhausted but she also didn't want to see people who would ask questions about her missing husband. Ironically, though, home wasn't safe; it was the most poignant reminder of all that she was an abandoned wife.

As it was for Ted and Madge, so it is for all spouses whose mates desert. The abandoned spouses, abandoned families, become immediately disrupted — plunged into bewildering crisis. In that sense sudden departure is akin to sudden death. One day everything is normal. The next day a person crucial in the lives of others has disappeared. Of course, death is final while abandonment need not be so, and many stay-behind husbands and wives do nurse the hope that their mates will have a change of heart and return.

Others are so infuriated, either by the disappearance or by the events that preceded it, that they say, "I'm glad she's gone," or, "Good riddance to that bastard!" Yet even fury doesn't altogether mitigate other painful feelings — of loss, of hurt.

"The family is in crisis," Harry N. Zelinka of the Family Service of Los Angeles stresses, "and the spouse who's left behind goes into a personal crisis."

The word for deserted spouses is *confused.* Their well-ordered world, at least their familiar, recognizable world, becomes disordered, strange. For many persons this is a time of panic; their normal defenses break down. The extent to which this breakdown occurs clearly varies from person to person. Like Ted, some can't manage even simple decisions in the first several days. Like Madge, some do strange things — behave hysterically in certain ways — during the initial period of abandonment. Sleep becomes a near-impossibility because of their intense anxiety, and, in a familiar vicious circle, the heightened anxiety lessens their ability to fall asleep. This circle overlaps another, equally vicious, one: the abandoned spouses are depressed as well as anxious; exhaustion from lack of sleep heightens their depression, and their depression makes them all the more exhausted.

Abandoned, Rejected, Hopeful — and Very Angry

Inevitably, left-behinds feel worthless.

Even spouses who say, "Good riddance!" know they've been rejected in the cruelest of ways, and it shows, it hurts. Abandoned spouses are quite apt to see themselves as ugly, as failures, maybe even as deserving the bitter fate that's theirs. They feel sorry for themselves. They envy other spouses who haven't been abandoned. And these other feelings bring on intense anger, rage and bitterness towards the deserters. How could they not harbor these hateful feelings toward the ones who have left them with so many serious problems?

Most terrifying of all for the left-behinds is not being sure any more of who they are or what kind of world they're living in. The familiar has become unfamiliar. They feel they've lost control over their lives.

Clearly, not everybody who has been abandoned feels these various emotions with the same passion. Some are more hurt than others. Some are more clear about what is going on inside them than are others. Some are better able to cope than are others. Generally, the more self-sufficient people are, the easier it is for them to deal with crisis situations of any kind. But since many of the left-behinds as well as many of the runaways have always been highly dependent, they don't have much self-sufficiency to draw upon. At least not at first. One young woman whose husband ran away when their baby was barely six months old couldn't sleep alone for the first few weeks; her mother and sister had to take turns being with her at night. It wasn't the dark she was afraid of; what so badly frightened her were her suicidal impulses.

The hope of an early return on the part of the runaway is nearly irresistible for some. Hope turns to fantasy. A husband whose wife took off shortly after their last child left for college recalls, "The first week after she left I dashed to the phone every time it rang, and ran to the front door whenever somebody came to call — I was utterly convinced that it was my wife wanting to come back. To be forgiven. But it never was her. Not for three months it wasn't. And when she did call it was to ask for a divorce."

How people deal with abandonment generally reflects the way they deal with any serious crisis. Some withdraw; they want to see no one, they shut themselves up at home. Some become restless, agitated; they engage in random movement and activities. They quit jobs, take jobs, date frenetically, break up with their dates, constantly visit relatives and friends. Some are models of dogged cheerfulness, and hearing how brave they are temporarily soothes their wounds. Some cry a lot, some get very drunk; many deny the agony they feel.

Feelings denied are feelings repressed, feelings repressed are feelings that will surface in destructively roundabout ways. The wife who denies to herself how enraged she is by her runaway husband is apt to take out her anger on her children (especially the male children). The husband who doesn't acknowledge to himself how bitter he feels toward his runaway wife is apt to take out all that anger on himself, which will bring him into a heavy, painful depression.

To deny feelings is to deny the reality of the situation. One way of denying reality is to cast blame. Blame can be cast outward: "It's all his (her) fault." Blame can be directed inward: "It's all my fault; if only I'd been a better person none of this would have happened." The truth is that in any runaway situation all parties concerned played their parts, grossly or subtly. Throwing blame is like throwing mud; it obscures the vision and keeps one from seeing what is really going on.

Another way of denying reality and avoiding the issues is to cast doubt on the sanity of the runaway spouse. The husband who does something like that — and it is more often stay-behind husbands rather than wives who seem to — is reacting passively in the runaway situation. Emotionally it gets him off the hook. Since she's crazy, he bears no responsibility for her act. He doesn't have to deal with his feelings of anger toward her. And he doesn't have to think about how to manage for himself, either.

Counselors who work with abandoned spouses suggest the following: you're going to be subject to all kinds of extreme and contradictory feelings. Acknowledge them, recognize them as "normal" under the circumstances. Try not to withdraw from life; instead, reach out to people. Accept the emotional support and physical help they give you. This is your time of need, so give to yourself by allowing others to give to you. Consider the help a family service or similar counseling agency might offer you — help in dealing with your emotions in this crisis, in handling the children, in arranging appropriate practical support services such as homemaker services.

How to Plan

There are so many problems to be faced, so much planning to be done. Who is going to support us now that my husband has run away? Who is going to take care of the kids now that my wife has gone? How will the children get to school? Who will look after them in the afternoons? This list goes on and on. The easiest thing to do is feel *overwhelmed*. Many left-behind spouses feel exactly that. "They implode with anxiety. They're buried under and then feel they can do nothing," says a social worker at the Family Service of Los Angeles.

There is an old mental health trick one can use to keep from feeling overwhelmed, or buried or imploded with anxiety: don't try to cope with all those problems at the very same time. You can't — nobody can — solve everything at once, and the attempt to do so brings on the feeling that one can solve *nothing*. Instead, establish priorities. Work on one problem at a time. Is the care of the children the most pressing problem? Then arrange with a relative, friend or homemaker service (either privately or through a social service agency) to provide for their temporary care. Getting professional help for that energy-draining depression may be at the top of the list.

Specifics vary from individual case to individual case. But one thing holds true for almost everyone: just the process of arranging priorities and getting to work on the first one can be tremendously strengthening. Counselors suggest: Acknowledge to yourself that you *are* coping, pat yourself on the back for the strengths you do show; *be good to yourself.*

And counselors suggest: think now in these early days of abandonment about your family of origin, your parents and close relatives. They can make you feel less alone, less abandoned. They can offer practical help. It is true that adult children who reach out to their parents in a marital crisis may not find the process an unmixed blessing. Those mothers and fathers may now go into vitriolic tirades against the deserting spouse, whom they've never really liked, anyway. They may rush into the breach, taking over, treating their deserted child like a child again. This is called infantilization. And the grown-up child, having suffered this grievous loss, may just want to succumb to being dealt with like a baby. It is something to be wary of. For all the pitfalls, though, during the crisis of abandonment even a controlling parent may be better than no parent at all.

And counselors advise: don't quit your job. Don't give up on the structures you've built for yourself, on the familiar people and routines that shape your life. Take full advantage of all the "support systems" you can muster — family, work, friends. Look into self-help groups — for instance, single-parent groups — for additional support.

Helping the Children Adjust

Boys and girls of whatever age need plenty of help in adjusting to the situation. Not only the spouse has been abandoned. So have they.

They're anxious. They're afraid. "I have yet to see a situation where there has been a separation or divorce, let alone a desertion, where there wasn't a very strong reaction on the part of the child," Naumi Alcalay points out.

The fact of its abruptness — that there has been no preparation or planning for it — makes desertion even harder to assimilate than separation or divorce. Like the deserted adult, the deserted child is buffeted by a variety of difficult and contradictory emotions. The abandoned child, like the abandoned adult, sees a frightening future. Unless the deserting parent has been extremely brutal physically or emotionally, the child nurses a compelling fantasy that the parent will suddenly return. The child feels the hurt of gross rejection and a pervasive sense of guilt. As a recently abandoned seven-year-old beautifully articulated this guilt, "If I'd been a good girl all the time Daddy wouldn't have gone away." The guilt is intensified if the child has ever imagined the deserting parent hurt or dead or otherwise gone — and what child hasn't imagined that at some time or other?

Finally, there is rage brought on by those feelings of rejection and guilt. Children who have had a reasonably good relationship with their deserting parent and get along badly with the remaining one may even have some sympathy for the one who departed. But that sympathy is alloyed with hurt and anger and bewilderment.

Older children are often able to do a fairly good job of sorting out these various feelings. For younger ones the pain is often so great they pretend the missing parent isn't gone at all. A five-year-old girl, whose father was missing for three weeks, still insisted that he came home from the office each evening. "And he kisses me goodnight when I go to bed," she swore.

Not surprisingly, abandoned children act in disturbed and disturbing ways. Boys are apt to get into fights with schoolmates or into arguments with teachers. They may cut school or strike up friendships with kids their parents would regard as undesirable. Vandalism is another way by which they express their hurt. One eleven-year-old boy broke fourteen windows in his school, each with methodical care, two days after his father deserted. Girls are more prone to act up inside their homes — becoming surly and argumentative — than on the outside.

How children react depends on their age, emotional make-up, maturity, which parent has gone and the kind of relationship they have had with that parent and the stay-behind. A six-year-old boy who, in the normal course of his development, wants his mother all to himself, will feel her disappearance much more keenly than the sixteen-year-old boy already half out of the nest. A thirteen-year-old girl is apt to have a terrible time adjusting to her father's disappearance; in terms of her development she is undergoing a replay of her own six-year-old stage when she wanted Daddy all to herself. The early adolescent girl whose father has run away often reacts by becoming sexually promiscuous or responding to boys in an unstable way. Older or younger, if the abandoned daughter was Daddy's favorite and Daddy is the one who runs, she may react by becoming terribly angry with her mother, putting all the blame on the mother.

If Mother runs away the trauma for children of both sexes is of a different nature. Their sense of security is profoundly shaken — especially in the case of the younger children — since it is generally Mother who feeds, clothes, supervises the children, who plays the nurturing role.

Sometimes abandoned parents are so caught up in their own troubles it doesn't occur to them that their children are in torment, too. Theirs is a comforting rationalization: "The less said about the disappearance, the better." Actually, the less said, the more confused abandoned children become. Again, this is particularly true of younger children. The less they know about what's going on, the more freely they're likely to give reign to their terrible fantasies in which they torment themselves with blame for having caused the missing parent's disappearance.

"It's best to explain as well as you can what has happened and what's happening now," counsels Judy Lang of New York City's Jewish Family Service. "Even children three or four years old can understand something." An important point: the discussion should be on a level the child *can* understand. Ms. Lang's suggestion is to begin with the simple fact that the child's father — or mother — has left. An anguished parent may find even that hard to do, but in the long run it is best for everybody concerned. Also important: stress that the parent's disappearance is *not* the child's fault, nor the fault of the remaining parent.

"Your father went away suddenly without telling us," one mother told her two small children, five and seven. "He had some problems he just felt he had to run from." The five-year-old said, "Oh." He seemed to understand, or at least was satisfied with the explanation. The seven-year-old asked, "Well, is he ever going to come back?" The mother's honest reply was, "Darling, I just don't know."

What she said was, after all, the truth. It is vital for parents to be truthful when discussing the desertion with their children. Counselors offer these guidelines: you certainly don't want to go into great detail, you don't want to be graphic about the reason for the desertion, but what you do say should be accurate. It is not accurate to say a missing mother or father has "died" when the fact is that the parent has run away. Even the youngest child will eventually find out the facts, be doubly horrified to learn them suddenly from some outside source, and be dismayed by the stay-behind parent's lie.

Be candid about the fact that you feel hurt and angry — children are quick to pick up feelings — but don't go on to downgrade the absent parent. The children are going to have a difficult enough time of it without being put in a position of having to choose sides, as well. Encourage the children to express their own feelings. Couple the anger the children feel with a correction of their terrible fantasy that they were responsible for his running away. Paint the runaway not as a good person or a bad person but as a human being who struggles and has assets and liabilities like everybody else — a person who has limitations but has contributed to the child's welfare, and whose own problems and liabilities have become too overwhelming. More than likely, unless the runaway was a real monster, that is more or less the truth.

Overcoming False Hopes, False Images

The tendency of left-behind parents may be to think, and to say to their children, "Don't worry, your father/mother will come back soon." It is a fantasy many abandoned spouses nourish. It is one most children cherish. And it is true that most runaways do return home within a few weeks. But most doesn't mean all. There is no guarantee *this* one will.

Though it is only natural, during the initial abandonment

period, to cling to the return fantasy, it does no good to continue to live as if the deserting spouse is about to walk in the front door. All it does is relegate one's life — and the kids' lives — to limbo.

A suburban Chicago woman whose husband took off wouldn't let anyone else mow the lawn because he always did it; the lawn became a mass of tangled weeds. Another abandoned wife refused to let the children sit in her husband's leather chair, even though he had been gone two months, because he never let them sit in it. Such approaches perpetuate the deserter's memory, make him a tangible presence in the home, promote the feeling that this is only a temporary situation — and impede the painful but necessary process of separation for both the left-behind spouse and the left-behind children.

The way to help oneself and the children, social workers advise, is to accept the situation as final, to define one's life in terms of being without that person and to deal with the return if and when it happens as a separate issue.

None of this is easy. In fact, it is very hard. Merely to talk about such troublesome feelings as anger and hurt is difficult in a family in which a desertion has taken place, since such families are least likely to have had an easy flow of communication among their members. And what about the left-behind parents' own preoccupations, angers, hurts, anxieties? How can they *not* have the urge to portray the runaway as a villain? How can they be expected to give extra love, attention, insight and reassurance to their children when they themselves are in such need of these things? So they may feel, realistically, that too much is being asked of them, all the more so if they aren't being shored up by crisis counseling.

Still, this advice can serve as a loose guideline to action, if not as step-by-step instruction, in how the abandoned parent and other family members who rally around may best help the abandoned child.

When to Locate and When to Let Go

Should deserted spouses look for their runaway mates? If so, how can they go about it? Is it sometimes best just to let things go?

Sometimes it is. Sarah and Peter do not make the ideal love story, but they illustrate the point. They met in a Nazi concentration camp, survived, married in Germany after the war, emigrated to the United States, had five children. The holocaust had taken its toll of Peter, however; he slipped in and out of mental institutions. A sallow, wraith-like figure, he seemed unconnected to reality. He babbled to himself, wore sandals in the snow, lived by himself in a tent in New Jersey for several months and didn't always recognize his kids. He disturbed and frightened them, and tormented his wife. He wasn't violent but he was a constant disruption to his family.

And then he ran away, and stayed away. Sarah, who had already been working closely with a family service agency, asked, "Should I find him?"

The answer was unequivocal: "We feel you should let him go."

In such cases, where the runaway spouse has shown an unremitting pattern of physical and mental abuse, the attitude among counselors generally is not to mount a search party.

On the other hand, some left-behinds feel that if they could only talk to their runaway spouses things would be okay. Some want to spit in their eyes. Some want them to clean up financial messes they left behind. Some want them to resume their marital and parental "duties." Some want alimony or child support or legal divorces.

Whatever the reasons, many left-behind spouses obviously wish they could track down their deserters. But how do they go about it?

Locating a runaway spouse may be as simple as asking the runaway's mother or siblings. Sometimes relatives condemn the runaway for running, sympathize with the abandoned one, and are willing to reveal all they know. Realistically, though, it more often works out the other way: they know but aren't willing to tell. Just as often the runaway doesn't tell his family of origin anything, at least initially.

How about going to the police? A missing persons report may be filed, but so what? No police department will send out an all points bulletin or assign a team of detectives to the case. The fact is that aside from small-town policemen who occasionally do local citizens a personal favor, police departments simply won't take on runaway-spouse cases. Why not? Because it isn't a crime to run away as such. As Sergeant Dean Thomas of the Los Angeles Police Department's Missing Persons Unit puts it, "Every person who's not a minor has the constitutional right to go where he wishes."

There are exceptions. For instance, the New York City Police Department will accept missing-spouse cases when the spouse who's gone is retarded (because the mentally retarded can't take care of themselves), or over sixty-five (on the supposition that the missing person might be senile), or where there's a suggestion of an involuntary disappearance (since a crime may have been committed), or when there's the possibility of suicide. Even if they take on a case that starts out as being one of possible foul play, they'll drop it immediately upon finding out that it's a simple runaway-spouse case. And even if they've located the missing spouse under such circumstances, they won't reveal that person's whereabouts. Other police departments follow a similar routine.

Government Help

Spouses have a constitutional right to flee, but they definitely do not have the right to leave their children destitute. Abandonment in that sense is a crime, and police officers will accept the complaint and refer it or the complainant to the local district attorney's office. Over the years, district attorneys have been far too swamped with murder, rape, grand larceny and other such cases to bother much with breadwinners who skip out on their responsibilities to their families.

But as welfare rolls have swollen, in 1975 the federal government created a new investigative entity — the Parent Locator Service (administered under HEW's Social and Rehabilitation Service). Each state is mandated to set up its own parent locator service (though some, like Massachusetts and Minnesota, have had theirs operating independently for a few years). Parent Locator Service is supposed to do just what its name says — track down absentee parents who have a responsibility for the support of their children.

What does all this mean to the stay-behind spouse? The abandoned one can now marshal the government's vast resources to help locate the deserter and make him pay.

The procedure is uncomplicated. Say Mr. Smith has fled his unhappy home, and Mrs. Smith and their three young children are made unhappier still by the fact that he left nothing in their joint bank account and she doesn't have a job. Mrs. Smith's first step is to contact the state or local child support agency in her area; this usually turns out to be the welfare department or the district attorney's office. There she fills out a background questionnaire that asks a number of questions about the runaway spouse. She pays a fee (around $20; had she been on welfare the service would have been free), and certifies that she is looking for this spouse for the purpose of collecting child support.

Now the investigation gets under way. It starts on the local level: the runaway's last employer is interviewed; the Post Office is checked to see if there's a forwarding address. If nothing turns up, on to the state level: computer checks are made with the state unemployment department, motor vehicles bureau, income tax bureau, and the like. Even Citizen's Band license files are now tapped. If the investigation still draws a blank, the state activates its computer link with the Parent Locator Service in the nation's capital. Parent Locator Service taps the Social Security Administration, the Internal Revenue Service, the Department of Defense and other agencies, all for the purpose of trying to locate the runaway's present whereabouts. If he is located, Mrs. Smith is notified; court action can follow, and if he doesn't pay what he owes in child support, a contempt citation or a writ of garnishment can be served on him.

Federal statistics show that about seventy-five percent of all absentee breadwinners are still living in the same state or county as the families they abandoned. If they aren't in the same state any more they can still be made to pay under the long-established Reciprocal Support of Dependents Law. Under this law a deserter can't escape his financial obligations to his family simply by moving to another state. It gives the spouse who is owed support the right to petition the court in the other state to summon the deserter for a hearing.

This federal program was brand-new as of mid-1976 and it may be years before it works with any real efficiency. Some of the states have been far behind schedule in setting up their programs to meet federal requirements. Some federal agencies lag in computerizing the data that facilitates a search. And court procedures can be used by the delinquent, even if he is located, to avoid making support payments for many months.

Private Agencies

Some left-behind spouses who are eager enough and can afford it — and many who can't — hire private detectives. The chapter that follows discusses their advantages and drawbacks in detail, but there is no reason why stay-behind spouses can't do some preliminary detective work on their own. Private detectives interview friends and relatives; stay-behind spouses can do that. (Caution: Left-behind wives should avoid telling their landlords that their husbands have run away. Nervous landlords have been known to start eviction proceedings, fearing loss of rental income.) Private detectives sometimes go through the runaway's personal effects, looking for clues; stay-behind spouses can do that, too. A deserted wife may, for instance, scour her deserting husband's dresser drawers, his night table, his basement workshop, the wastepaper basket he last used and so on. She'll be looking for a travel voucher or folder, or some information from a chamber of commerce in another city. He might have left a telltale letter carelessly behind. Business papers should be carefully examined. In any event, she'll probably need his Social Security number, credit card numbers, union data and similar information at some point after he leaves.

Needless to say, the same advice holds true for stay-behind husbands whose wives have deserted them.

An agency that wants all the information it can get is New York City's Family Location and Legal Services — the old National Desertion Bureau under a new name. As part of Jewish Family Service, it is nonsectarian and its moderate fees are arranged on a sliding scale depending on the family's earnings.

How Family Location and Legal Services works can be instructive to anyone who wants to go about looking for a missing spouse. It asks for a complete description on the runaway: physical characteristics, health problems, birthmarks, occupational history, organizational history, financial aspects, military records, criminal records, detail of car ownership and other such data. It also wants names and addresses of the runaway's friends and relatives and of any "other man" or "other woman" who may have been on the scene.

It routinely checks motor vehicle records; the expiration date on the driver's license is especially significant because at some point it has to expire. Once it does, another check is made; if the request to the New York State Department of Motor Vehicles comes back "no record," it is reasonable to assume the runaway has left the state.

Various police departments and the United States Passport Division are checked, since some runaways leave the country. A number of deserters of Jewish extraction have headed for Israel. One runaway husband took his two children and ran off to Budapest, Hungary. He was located there; his wife flew to Budapest and waited two months, hanging around the address the agency had supplied her, until she finally spotted her children. Then she had to wait some more, until they were alone, at which time she hustled them to the United States embassy. Finally she managed to fly them back to the United States.

Since many of the families that apply to Family Location and Legal Services are working-class, the absentee spouses are apt to hold union cards. The agency routinely checks with unions when this is appropriate; unions are generally cooperative in supplying relevant information. One runaway wife was located in Miami because she was still paying dues to her union, even though she wasn't working, so she wouldn't lose her pension plan.

Desertion Divorces

No matter who looks for them, or how effectively, a minority of runaway spouses can't be located nor do they return of their own volition. They're just there, settled or unsettled, presumably content to lead whatever lives they're leading as runaway spouses. Does that mean their left-behind husbands or wives are stuck in a matrimonial limbo? Does it mean they have to wait a long time, seven years or so, before they can be legally free?

Neither.

Desertion constitutes grounds for divorce. The trick lies in *proving* desertion. In many states the deserted party has to demonstrate that a "good-faith" search to find the missing spouse actually was made. A lawyer is needed. (Some mental health agencies also provide legal and paralegal services.) In New York, as in many other states, a summons can be served on the defendant — the deserter — either through "alternative service" or by "publication."

Alternative service occurs when the judge on the case allows the summons to be served by mail at the defendant's last known address. Publication means a search made via newspaper ads in a local paper — an ad that goes something like this: "Has anybody seen John Jones, 5'11", 175 lbs. . . .?" The ad has to run a prescribed number of days. If an actual physical search for the deserter is made, the attorney handling the case presents to the court an affidavit that outlines how long the defendant has been missing and lists where a search for him has been conducted — among relatives, church members, last employer, police departments and so forth.

Judges vary in the amount of proof they want. Some require publication *and* evidence of search. Also a factor is the length of time the defendant has been missing. Many judges demand at least a year's absence, some a longer period. But in time no deserted spouse needs to remain "deserted," regardless of whether or not the spouse who ran ever shows up again.

"I Want to Come Home"

Fortunately most left-behind spouses don't have to go through such procedures. In the majority of runaway spouse cases the missing husbands or wives are located or, more likely, return of their own volition.

Suddenly the earlier fantasy becomes a reality. Suddenly there's that phone call or letter. Or a tentative approach, made from the abandoner to the abandoned, through a relative or friend. The runaway wants to come home.

What then?

Even if the left-behind spouse has the impulse to shout, "Yes! Yes!," even if the contact brings on a rush of joy, things rarely turn out to be that simple. The other feelings — hurt, anger, disappointment, mistrust — can't be discounted. Nor can the fact of abandonment. The negative feelings may unaccountably even intensify, and bring on a rush of rage.

One wife whose husband reappeared after having been gone for three months recalls, "He stood there on the doorstep, a silly, sheepish grin on his face, holding a scruffy suitcase in one hand and kind of reached out to me with the other. My heart leaped to my throat at the sight of him, but then I heard myself making this awful sound, like it expressed all the shit, all the misery, he'd put me to. And then I didn't know myself, I went wild — cursing him, hitting him, right out there on the front porch where all the neighbors could see and hear. I didn't care, didn't care."

Returning runaways often are unprepared for such violent reactions. They aren't equipped to anticipate the enormity of what they've done. But left-behind spouses who have had to deal with being profoundly rejected, with the rejected and frightened children, and with the angry creditors may not care to don the mantle of magnanimity the other has fashioned.

The runaway's return can have many different effects. Some runaways come back only to put their lives in order through legal separation or divorce — possibly because they have met other potential mates. Some left-behind spouses have themselves used the runaway's absence to assess their marriages and to conclude that they're not worth saving. Some do want to try to save their marital relationships but not at the cost of returning to the old marital patterns.

People do change and draw strength from the process of changing. For instance, it is not at all uncommon for highly dependent wives — the kind who married at seventeen — to pick up the pieces of their lives sometime after their husbands have run, to find jobs for themselves, to become more self-confident, to become eager to take care of themselves rather than to have *men* take care of them. This is a slow process, it may take quite a bit of counseling or therapy, but it occurs. For that matter, there are runaway spouses who also have changed significantly during their absences, resolving not to be trapped again by old, destructive marital patterns. None of this happens often, but it happens.

More frequently the stay-behind spouse has one "agenda" — as the mental health people like to call a half-conscious or unconscious program of action — the returned spouse another. And sometimes the returned spouse expects complete forgiveness, while the left-behind spouse intends to keep the runaway in a state of perpetual and abject contrition. That kind of welcome home hardly promises a happy ending in the sense of an improved marriage. What it does is to create a relationship as unbalanced as what went before.

That is one possibility. Another involves the returned runaway's attempts to get his or her own way. However it may be expressed verbally, the unconscious thinking goes something like this: "See how strongly I felt about things? Strongly enough to run away. See how strongly I feel about you? Strongly enough to come back. Now will you do as I say?" Manipulation may not be — probably isn't — anything new in this person's life; it's the customary way he or she deals with the world. But it does not further the cause of happy marriage.

Anger is another stumbling block on the road to better marital times. There has to be a lot of it in the air at first. No escape from that. Better to face it, to deal with it, to get it over with. Avoidance won't work, as Alan and Susan, a middle-aged Los Angeles couple, discovered. Alan ran away; he came back after nearly a month's absence. Susan was furious with him, but couldn't express her fury. Instead, on the surface, she was all smiles: "I'm so happy you're back, darling." Meanwhile, she was sniping at him fiercely. Little digs, snide comments about him to the children, reaching out to him physically, sexually, then suddenly tightening up. She honestly couldn't help herself.

What was going on with Susan? She wasn't expressing her negative feelings, and she wasn't getting what she wanted. What she really wanted was *not* to have Alan home but to have them live apart for a while, to see how things went. But since she couldn't express "not nice" feelings directly, she couldn't tell him the truth. Yet she couldn't control her circuitous expressions of anger, either.

This is only part of their story. Alan, too, had his difficulties with anger. Anger was something he could never tolerate from his wife (which made it that much harder for her to speak up) either before the runaway episode or afterward.

Both spouses were in collusion. Both pretended to feel no anger, no hostility. It stopped them from working out the problems of their marriage. Under the circumstances the inevitable happened: they broke up.

Trust and Meaning

Two basic issues have to be resolved if the reunion is to lead to a happier, healthier marriage. The first is *trust*. The second is *the meaning of the runaway episode*.

By running, the runaway has obviously violated trust. But lack of trust is nobody's exclusive prerogative — the one who ran may also feel, strongly and justifiably, mistrust of his mate. Whenever there is a split in a relationship, be it separation, divorce or running away, trust is *always* a sensitive issue at the time reconciliation is being contemplated. As Thomas Waner of the Family Service of Los Angeles puts it, "They can both be very mature people and say, 'I want you and you want me and we love each other' — but the reestablishment of a sense of trust that makes one feel safe is difficult and takes a long time."

Reestablishing trust is one piece of "work." Understanding the meaning of the runaway episode is another. If the episode is to make a constructive difference in their lives the two partners have to be willing to talk about it in searching, rather than accusatory, terms.

Some germane questions: why did the runaway run? What did running away mean to him or to her? What did the runaway learn from the experience? What meaning did the act of running have for the abandoned mate? Does the left-behind really understand what prompted the other to commit this emotionally violent act?

Ron Johnson of the Family and Children's Service of Minneapolis sums up: "The two partners should ask themselves and each other, 'What does the runaway act represent in terms of what we really need to look at and deal with?'"

How to Help the Children

Caught up in their own rush of confusing and conflicting emotions, parents frequently forget that the children also are profoundly ambivalent about the meaning of the runaway's return. The reunion is just as hard on them. No matter how much they might want that parent back, they have their own angers and hurts to contend with. They *were* abandoned. They *did* feel utterly rejected. So in part they have to feel hostile about the runaway's return — which doesn't need to stop them from feeling glad, as well.

To some extent, how hostile children are toward the returned runaway parent also depends on what the home atmosphere was like before that parent took off. If there had been a lot of tension, which abated somewhat with the runaway's departure, their hostility is apt to be fairly intense. If there was warmth and love before, they aren't likely to be as hostile. Wendy, who is sixteen, was frankly relieved when her father ran off, because he drank heavily and created violent scenes. Upon his return Wendy expected things to be as bad as they were, and she'd had enough. So she ran away. Calling from a friend's house two days later, she said, "I won't come back as long as the old man's there." She was sent to stay with relatives. Bernice, who is the same age, wept bitterly and shut herself in her room when her runaway father returned. Her parents conferred and decided to leave her alone for a while. They understood her upset and were hoping she would work things out for herself. Late the next day she came downstairs and hugged and kissed her father. He broke down and cried. She cried. *A bond was reforged.*

Counselors advise: help your children to explore their feelings about the runaway parent's return — both their negative and positive feelings. Don't negate their anger, don't be punitive about it, don't make them suppress it: they have as much right and as much need to express hostility as the adults in the situation do.

Suggestions for the returned parent: be prepared for some rejection on your children's part, at least until they've worked through their angry feelings and adjusted to the new situation to an extent. It is very hard to accept rejection from one's own boys and girls, but remember that it's just as hard for them to be rejected by their parents. And they were, in the sense that you ran away from them, too. Meeting their rejection with hurt, anger or hostility only worsens the situation; reverse roles in your mind and imagine how you would feel if you were they. Be patient. Be understanding. If you are, they are likely to come around.

Because of the difficult emotions a reunion engenders, it might be best all around to avoid a precipitous return home. Some counselors suggest allowing a couple of weeks or so, from the time the runaway first contacts his family to the time he actually returns home. This would be in the nature of a preparation period — for everyone involved to think about the various issues, to get the kids ready for the reunion, to begin to deal with the various problems. Possibly the runaway could stay somewhere nearby while "negotiations" are proceeding.

Caseworkers at the Family Service of Los Angeles told of Bernie, a runaway husband, and his successful homecoming. Mounting debts precipitated mounting marital conflicts between Bernie and his wife, Edie. Finally he couldn't take it any more and ran. He went from Los Angeles to San Diego. There he supported himself by driving a cab. When his panic subsided, Bernie began to miss his family. At last his yearning for Edie and his two young children, his girl and his boy, grew too strong. Through a close friend he sent out feelers: would Edie be receptive to a telephone call directly from him? Yes, she would be. He called. They talked haltingly, as if one wrong word on either's part would suddenly break the connection.

He said, "I want to come home."

She said, "I want you home, but I need a little more time."

He was disappointed but said he guessed he understood.

They talked a few more times in the ensuing weeks — tentative, exploratory talks. Once he also had a few awkward words with his children.

At last, about a month after his first phone call, Edie said, "Bernie, please come home. I want you, the children want you. It's not going to be easy, but we want you with us."

Bernie agreed it wouldn't be easy. The next day he left San Diego and went back to his family. Upon his return home nobody fell into his arms. Nobody said, "Let's forget this ever happened." The family went into therapy. They began to struggle with all those hard, contradictory feelings that are inevitable under the circumstances. But they felt a sense of guarded optimism, too. Slowly, cautiously, they were at last report turning something unfortunate into something good. The prognosis on the part of the counselors was that this runaway had returned home to stay home.

Bringing in the Bloodhounds: How Private Investigators Track Runaways

No Guarantees

Mr. Keen, Tracer of Lost Persons, was a miracle worker. Every week, on the popular old radio serial, he found his man, or woman or child. He tracked them down relentlessly and with spectacular ingenuity. Real life isn't a radio script, however, even if it sometimes seems like a bad soap opera, and successes don't come so frequently. How often they do come is anybody's guess. Private investigators, whether they work for supermarket chains like Pinkerton's or Burns International Security Services, or run a corner-grocery type of operation, don't like to talk about their failures.

How good are private eyes in finding runaways? That depends on their leads, their contacts, their perseverance, their cleverness, on how lucky they are, and on how good they are in taking advantage of lucky breaks. Some self-styled Sam Spades insist that, given enough time and money, anybody in hiding can be found. That is self-serving non-sense. On the other hand, unless a runaway is constantly and cold-bloodedly dedicated to the task of remaining in hiding, a persevering detective can eventually track him or her down.

Library vs. Field Work

How do private investigators work in finding someone who has dropped from sight? They use a variety of methods. One example is Ed Goldfader, the president of Tracers Company of America, Inc. Founded in 1924, and with a network of about 300 operatives and correspondents around the country, New York City-based Tracers serves lawyers, banks and educational institutions, as well as individuals who want to locate missing relatives.

Whether he is looking for missing spouses or stockholders, Goldfader's pride is the Tracers library — a repository for telephone directories ancient and current from all over the country, city directories ancient and modern, listings from professional organizations and social registers of all kinds. It's an astonishing hoard of reference materials on the past and present whereabouts and activities of over fifty million U.S. residents.

Goldfader claims, "Not only can we find out where an individual we're seeking was living, but who was in the same household, who lived next door."

Another example is John C. Hall, founder of Securities Unlimited, a Los Angeles-based private investigative agency. Hall looks like a man who would rather be out stalking the runaway than combing old telephone directories for leads. According to his modest brochure, he was a licensed heli-copter and fixed-wing pilot and served with the Army Special Forces intelligence section and the Los Angeles City

Police Department before becoming a private eye. Unlike Tracers, which specializes in missing persons, Securities Unlimited offers a shopper's delight of investigative services — surveillance, domestic relations work, narcotics investigations, accident and fraud investigations, lie detector and guard services. And, of course, it hunts the missing.

How to Stay Missing Forever

"If I were to run away, I couldn't be found," says Hall. "I'd change my name, driver's license, cars, credit cards, everything. I'd have to sever completely all my past relationships."

Most runaways are unable — or unwilling — to make such an awesome break with the past. This is what leaves them vulnerable to exposure. For this very reason, then, Goldfader, Hall, and every other investigator worthy of his state license tries to elicit as much information as possible about the missing person before starting out on the chase. Goldfader asks clients to fill out a sixty-five-item form on the runaway, including questions on favorite sports, foods and hobbies. Hall says he spends an hour or two with each client, going over the minutiae of the missing person's life.

"People are creatures of habit," he stresses. This is the runaway spouse's Achilles' heel. The runaway husband thoughtlessly charges something on his old credit cards, the bridge-happy wife joins a bridge club wherever she lands, runaways with a passion for Mexican food head for Mexican restaurants in whatever towns they find themselves. A runaway husband's hunger for chicken mole did, in fact, catch him up. The investigator on the case pinpointed the town the man was staying in, but couldn't trace his home or business address. So he went to the town and, the runaway's photo in hand, talked to the proprietors of the three Mexican restaurants there. A ten-dollar bill made one of the owners come alert. Yes, the man in the photograph dined there every

Wednesday night. The following Wednesday the runaway did show up, dined leisurely, then unknowingly led the tailing investigator to his home. On Thursday morning the detective phoned the lawyer who'd hired him (on behalf of the runaway's wife) and gave him the information.

In one of Hall's cases a runaway wife's love for horses tripped her up. Annie had run from her family in Los Angeles and was missing for about three months. Among the things Annie's husband told Hall, when he hired him, was that Annie had trained horses professionally, had once owned her own horse, and badly missed horses. It was Hall's most promising lead. "I figured that now she'd be around horses somehow," he says. So he donned his riding boots, dressed up like a man who knows his way around stables, and made the rounds of the ranches in the Los Angeles area.

He told the stable people he was from the south and was a buyer and seller of horses. The lingo was no problem to him; over the years he has picked up enough information to be conversant about many occupations. But talking like a seasoned horse trader didn't get him anywhere for a while. At last, nosing around one of the stables, he came across one of those lucky breaks that investigators need. He saw pinned up on a wall a postcard from a woman who signed herself "Annie."

Hall hunted up the stable owner. He didn't mention seeing the card. What he said was that he was an occasional visitor to Los Angeles, that he'd known Annie, and that he'd been negotiating with her to buy a horse when she suddenly disappeared. "I was talking to her husband and he said she wanted this horse of mine real bad," he said. "I knew she used to ride out here and I was wondering if you've seen her or heard from her." The stable owner, disarmed, told Hall just where the runaway wife could be found.

Hall says of his approach, "If you come on the right way — if you forget you're an investigator, people tell you things.

If you go in saying who you are and what you really want, you get no cooperation."

On the Track of the Missing

Many investigators work on the assumption that someone in the runaway's immediate circle — a relative, a friend, a companion at work, a drinking buddy — knows where he is. They may not elicit the information, but they'll give it a try, or they should. Some have a policy of not going to relatives the left-behind spouse has already unsuccessfully questioned, others make the attempt anyway. J. M. Martin, another Manhattan-based private investigator whose specialty is missing persons, says that sometimes relatives do unwittingly give away the runaway's whereabouts — *if* a suitable pretext can be found.

When he begins an investigation Martin wants to know where the missing person used to hang out. Chances are slight the runaway will keep on going to that place, but someone there might have acted as his confidant. Martin located one runaway wife by having an operative go to the bar she frequented on her "woman's night out." The operative posed as a good friend of hers and got the information she was after.

Role-playing as a horse breeder, or a friend of the runaway, or whatever else might be suitable under the circumstances, is, in the parlance of the trade, to use a "pretext." Often this is the only way they can extract some salient bit of data. It also challenges their investigative ingenuity.

Most investigators don't like to go into much detail about the pretexts they use; it is something like a trade secret. And there is no point in alerting potential informants to your object. Posing as a friend, pretending the missing person is suddenly heir to an estate, acting in the guise of an insurance investigator, acting like a prospective employer — all are

common pretexts. Every investigator one meets swears up
and down he never poses as a cop or a government agent —
and, of course, impersonating a police officer or a government man could lead to a speedy revocation of license plus
a stiff jail sentence. But one would have to possess an un-
shakable conviction in the absolute moral purity of human
beings to believe that no private eye ever poses as a public
eye.

Private Access Data

Much of the information that the private eyes need comes
from public sources. Motor vehicle departments, for instance,
file drivers' licenses, which reveal drivers' addresses, descriptions, physical handicaps, whether they've been confined in
a jail or mental institution, and more. All loans made by
banks and finance companies are filed with county clerks
and become public records. City and county tax records
are public. Much of the information that is especially useful
in tracking missing persons can be gotten by establishing the
right contacts with somebody who has access to utility and
telephone subscriber data, employment agency records,
banking, credit card and insurance information. Every
investigator above the amateur level has at least one friend
who works in a credit-reporting agency.

Many runaways are discovered because they keep on using
their old credit cards, forgetting that duplicate copies of
receipts and bills will eventually be sent to the homes they
ran from. Some investigators — Goldfader, for one — are
convinced that such "forgetting" is actually an unconscious
way of asking to be found. It could also be that panic running isn't conducive to logical thinking. Too, the average
runaway may not be aware that credit card information can
be obtained almost instantaneously.

In fact, investigators are sometimes able to get almost

daily records of credit card transactions. This is how a
private detective in Las Vegas, hunting a runaway husband,
kept continuous track of him. The runaway made ample
use of his credit card and did a lot of traveling. The detective,
seeing the credit card rundown, was able to follow his every
move. For three months the fugitive spouse moved about —
to Los Angeles, San Francisco, San Diego, Kansas City,
North Dakota. The private eye spotted one interesting
charge in North Dakota — a hefty sum spent on flowers. He
contacted the flower shop and learned that the flowers had
been sent to a wedding chapel. This led to another intriguing
discovery: the runaway had committed bigamy by marrying
a young woman while still married to the detective's client,
the runaway's wife.

Credit card purchases can uncover a runaway long after
he has fled his home. In a striking case of this kind, a runaway husband bolted with $100,000. Nearly a year later he
was pinned down, in California, because he'd charged a $1.10
breakfast in a motor lodge.

Phone and Mail Traps

The telephone, too, has a way of exposing the runaway
who presumably doesn't want to be exposed. For instance,
Hall tries to turn those midnight phone calls that runaways
so often make to his own advantage.

"It's a psychological battle," he said. "You start working
on them, you start feeding them into it, you start getting
them to respond more to you."

He was referring to the way the left-behind spouse should
"handle" the runaway who is making the phone call. First
may come the silent call, the one during which the runaway
says nothing. Sound advice is to respond, "Darling, I know
it's you. Just say a few words, just a word so I can hear your
voice again." Sooner or later, driven by the need to com-

municate with home, the runaway will presumably break down and talk. This engenders some regular communication with the spouse who is left behind.

After the runaway has become hooked on those phone calls — after they've started to be an important event in the life of a fugitive — the left-behind spouse says, "I don't know if I'll be home tomorrow night when you're going to call. Just give me a phone number, even the number in a phone booth, if that will make you feel better about not being traced. I'll call you at ten o'clock, but please answer so I'll know you're there." The first attempt may bring a refusal. But as the runaway comes to count more and more on those calls home, he or she is apt to succumb and offer a phone number. Even if it is a number in a phone booth, it does a lot to narrow the geographical location. It provides the area code, and telephone company contacts can provide the location of the booth. Then, next time such a call is made, the investigator or his agent in that area can wait for the missing spouse to show up, and then, when the call is over, tail the runaway home.

Then there are the mails. If phone calls don't work out, the runaway may be persuaded to correspond with the abandoned spouse. Even one letter can give away the runaway's whereabouts. The abandoned one is instructed to say, or write, "I know you're running out of money, let me send you a few dollars — I'll send the money to a post office box, to general delivery, if you want."

The runaway thinks general delivery is fine. How could that lead the spouse at home to discover the new address? Feeling secure and grateful, the runaway goes to the post office to pick up the letter — and there is the investigator or a confederate, armed with a photo, ready to follow.

Depending on the complexity of the case and the amount of money the client is willing to spend on the search, an investigator might ask to inspect the premises from which the runaway took off. Dresser drawers, wastepaper baskets, the desk the runaway used may yield provocative results. A check of old phone bills might show toll or long-distance calls to unusual numbers — maybe a lover's number, maybe the number of a hotel somewhere.

One interesting case involved a businessman who was cheating on his wife. She was aware of his extramarital adventures but tolerated them. What she wouldn't tolerate was his request for a divorce; she said, in effect, "If you want it, it's going to cost you plenty."

Then, without warning, this husband moved out of the family home. His wife couldn't discover his new address. She was unable to get through to him at work and he kept shaking off the gumshoes she'd hired. Finally, private detectives made a thorough search of the house. One thing they examined minutely was the runaway's clothing, most of which he had left behind. They jotted down laundry markings and dry-cleaning tags. They noted that he used a chain laundry. Going from branch to branch, and showing the help there the husband's photo, they eventually got to the right one. When the man behind the counter saw the photo, he exclaimed, "Oh, he and his wife were just in, picking up the laundry." The "wife" was the businessman's lover, of course; they were living together now. The laundryman helpfully supplied his new address and soon his real wife was confronting him.

Payoffs

Laundry tags, reading material — everything is grist for the investigator's mill. In one of Hall's cases, involving a young wife who ran away, a magazine tripped her up. While examining the house from which she fled, he noticed that she had left a women's magazine behind. Flipping through it, he spotted an ad for YWCAs, with some cities and prices scribbled in. He put out a poster with her picture on it, offering a $50 reward for anyone who had information as to her whereabouts, and sent it to the Ys in question. Soon someone from a Y in a nearby city responded; the wife was staying there.

As one investigator says, "A night clerk working for two-fifty an hour will want that extra fifty bucks."

Rewards held out as bait for missing spouses, as for missing pets, are commonplace. Reward-offering circulars sent to shelters, free clinics and the like, for example, apparently do bring results. One investigator insisted that in the case of runaway wives he has also gotten positive results from women's centers. "Even though they say they won't rat on their sisters, there's always somebody who needs extra dough," he explained.

This investigator pointed out that homes and crash pads in which gay men stay are something else again — "very tight, very closed-mouthed; I've got contacts in some, but they're very selective about whom they'll rat on." Sometimes, his own gay informants never see a particular gay runaway, even if he's in the area. He remains well-hidden and protected.

Kids Are a Special Problem

If homosexuals are hard to find, teenagers are no easier. If an investigator finds half the youngsters he is asked to locate, he can consider himself a very sharp detective. By contrast, solving about seventy-five percent of his missing adults cases would be considered good work.

Several reasons account for the difficulty in finding runaway adolescents. One is that there's less to "exploit" in terms of their backgrounds. As Goldfader outlines the investigator's dilemma, "Just how much of a past history does a teenager have?" Not much. This diminishes the number of potential clues to the runaway's whereabouts. Too, when a teenager takes off his parents generally can't offer much in the way of leads; they just don't know where he might be. As for the teenage subculture, it tends, as we've seen, to be protective of its own. Some investigators in the business of trying to locate the missing do claim to have networks of informants — young people who will turn in other young people. One investigator claimed to have an informant in New York's East Village "who for the almighty dollar is willing to turn in anybody." But the teenage sub-culture is constantly shifting; adolescent informants do not, after all, either stay put in one place forever or remain perpetual teenagers. So those networks aren't stable.

Another difficulty: while adults are creatures of habit, to the delight of the investigators who look for them, young people are unpredictable in their actions. Moreover, parents often know relatively little about what's going on in their teenagers' lives. This is especially true in runaways' families, where relationships tend to be poor and communication problematic. What has the missing teenager's secret life been like? That is the question the private eye, if he is good, endeavors to answer. He presumes that in school, out of school, things have been going on in that teenager's life of which the parents are unaware.

This is borne out time and again. Suzie is a bright, pretty, fifteen-year-old. She lives in suburban Port Washington and takes the train to Manhattan every Saturday for her lessons at the Museum of Modern Art. But Greenwich Village entices her; after classes she sneaks into the Village to visit the leather shops and rap with the locals. Little by little she gets sucked into the seemingly glamorous Village life. And then one of the boys, to whom she's drawn, talks her into running away.

Karen is sixteen, a ravishing girl. Karen illustrates how teenagers, being far more mobile than most adults, can lead investigators on seemingly endless and very expensive chases. Karen was on drugs, something her divorced mother, with whom she was living in Los Angeles, knew nothing about until it was too late. One day Karen ran away. In time she began to send short notes home. Eventually a private detective was engaged to find her.

The first thing the detective did was to examine the postmarks on those notes. They were sent from Marin County, up north. He notified the appropriate police departments to detain the girl if they spotted her. Nothing. Then another note from Karen; she'd gotten a job in a restaurant in Portland, Oregon. The postmark on that note narrowed her location to a specific part of the city. The detective went to Portland accompanied by a female operative; pretending to be the runaway girl's parents, they scouted the area. There was good news and bad news: they found the hotel she had been staying in, but she'd left the day before.

Back in Los Angeles, the private eye fine-tooth-combed Karen's possessions, scrutinizing everything. Diaries, letters, notes — he went through them all in search of clues. At last he got a lead: Karen had been corresponding with a cousin in Chicago. He got on the phone and talked to this woman, who told him that Karen had been there but was gone again, this time to Tucson, Arizona, with a bunch of other teenagers she'd met. Then the detective circulated Karen's photo in Tucson and had her picked up. This story has an apparently happy ending; Karen agreed to live with her cousin in Chicago and hasn't run away again.

Caveat Emptor

The services of private investigators are costly. The client pays the tab for all expenses, of course, plus an hourly fee. Some investigators charge $15, some $20 or $25 per hour. Occasionally a flat fee is quoted. The hourly fee may not sound like much, except that an investigation can take ten hours, a hundred hours, or more. Goldfader's clients, for instance, pay from $500 to $2,500 to find their runaway relatives.

However, since clients pay by the hour, not by degree of success, a great deal of money can go in the detective's direction with the runaway still as elusive as before. Ethical private eyes keep their clients honestly abreast of what is happening, what new leads (if any) they have uncovered, whether or not something really tangible shows promise of turning up. That leaves it up to the clients to decide whether or not to continue the investigation.

Many of the people who hire private detective agencies to find their missing spouses, children or other relatives don't seem to know what they're getting into. They seem to believe that the intervention of a professional means the missing one will be found within a matter of a few days, if not hours. They plunk down a retainer, hoping for a quick find, then soon discover they've run out of money with which to carry on the pursuit.

Martin's experience may be typical. "Many can't afford to pay the tab if I should go for more than a week or so," he said. An investigator can often make a pretty good guess as to how long a particular investigation should take — based on the nature of the runaway case, the leads available and other factors. But that is not always possible, and not every private eye is necessarily honest in his estimate.

People hiring private investigators to find their missing aren't always told that, should the runaway suddenly come back on his own, no refund is forthcoming. The investigator — quite properly — justifies his bill in terms of the time he has put in. He can also claim that the runaway learned of his investigation somehow and became so frightened as a result that he hurried home. Occasionally that's a valid claim. Sometimes it is not. Because so many runaways do return home within a few weeks, some investigators will not accept a case until the subject has been gone for thirty days. Many other investigators take the opposite tack; the hotter the trail the better, is their rationale. Unless money is no issue, however, holding off for a month or so is probably a sound idea.

In shopping for a private investigator, *caveat emptor* should be the rule. Ethical investigators and police officers suggest the following: though you're likely to find dozens of private detectives listed in the Yellow Pages of the telephone directory, in this instance don't let your fingers do the walking for you. Investigate the investigator. Some investigators are masters at writing impressive reports that read like a detective story when in fact they barely lifted their feet off the desk in conducting the investigation. In runaway teenager cases, if no leads are handy, some merely send fliers to likely police departments — something parents can do on their own at a fraction of the cost. Some private investigators, even with years of experience in the business, have very little practice in missing persons work.

How *do* potential clients get their money's worth? It is not always easy, but a few precautions will help. Clients should make sure the private eye is city and/or state licensed; at least he then has met a minimum standard of bondability. Good bets are retired police or sheriff's department officers, or ex-FBI agents — *if* they were working in investigative capacities while in civil service. How long has the investigator been in business? How many missing persons has he traced? He may brag about the associations he belongs to; actually, they're less important than his experience as a tracer of missing persons. A check with the local Better Business Bureau will reveal whether any consumer complaints have been filed against the private detective being considered. If possible, hire the investigator on the recommendation of an attorney whom you trust, one who has used this investigator consistently and found him satisfactory.

On the other hand, people with limited financial resources

and slim or nonexistent leads to the runaway's current whereabouts shouldn't expect even the most qualified private detective to pull a missing relative out of his fedora. And even the most expert of detectives can, at best, only give an accurate rundown on the missing person's whereabouts and current activities. He can't *detain* the runaway. He can't bring the person back home, nor can he guarantee that a runaway who is located and returns home will stay home. (In many husband or wife runaway cases, investigators say, the end result is either another runaway episode or a divorce.)

In the case of runaway minors, once the detective locates them he can arrange to have them detained legally, but, again, he has no control over what happens after the parent-child contact is effected. He doesn't and can't be expected to control the factors that prompted the runaway episode in the first place. What happens after runaways are located is up to the runaways and the persons who paid to have them found.

Final Thoughts: Runaways Forever

Social Factors

We live in families, we live in the Family of Man. Our run-aways don't simply run from their families, from stresses and strains they personally experience there or elsewhere. What happens to them is played out against the backdrop of the larger "family" — that is, society.

In recent years the American family has been under enor-mous stress. It is obviously impossible here to enumerate all of the causes, but a few follow. Parents are expected to be all things to their growing offspring, to play the multitudinous roles that a whole collection of extended family members shared in the past. Pressured to buy and spend, spouses and parents overextend themselves financially. A great many breadwinners hold down two jobs (when they can get them); it is also one of the major factors bringing wives and mothers in ever-growing numbers out of the home and into the work-place. (About half of all mothers with children under eigh-teen are now working mothers.) Though families aren't moving as frequently as they did a few years back, we're still a nation of nomads. Traditional family supports — meaning-ful church membership, for one — are no longer as helpful as they once were. Yet today's family is faced with a bewilder-ing array of options. Sexual. Social. Recreational. Change — technological, economic, social — plays havoc with stability. In times past families could expect a reasonable amount of stability from decade to decade. Now it hardly seems realistic to expect anything to remain the same one year to the next. As a consequence of these various pressures, the number of single-parent families is growing inexorably; today four out of every ten marriages end in divorce. It is self-evident — and the runaway case histories presented in the previous chapters prove — that such factors play their part in bringing some people to the panic point of running.

Another causative factor: *rising expectations*. Everybody wants to be happy. Everybody wants to be self-realized, self-actualized. Frustrated wives want to be fulfilled. Bored workers want their jobs to have meaning. Adolescents claim their hedonistic rights. Singles seek the "good life." The aged want to feel useful, valued. The "pursuit of happiness" is no longer a statement of political philosophy or broad social in-tent but the credo by which we all individually — and deter-minedly — live. Everything suddenly becomes possible. The more we have, the more we want. Why, then, doesn't "it" come more quickly and more satisfyingly? Why aren't we more content with our lot? Rising expectations lead us to reject "settling" for anything. We want instant gratification in our ever-changing hurry-up world or we want out. And running away is one "out."

It seems evident that as long as such factors remain present in our imperfect surroundings, the runaway phenomenon will not only remain with us but the number of runaways, young and old, will increase.

Crisis Intervention for Youths

Some juvenile-runaway studies are disturbing in their conclusions. They show that adults who ran away as children turn out to be more emotionally disturbed, more given to heavy drinking, more drug-dependent, more prone to criminal behavior, than a comparable group of adults whose juvenile history doesn't include running away.

But there is more involved than bad kids turning into bad adults. They are troubled kids who run from troubled or failed families or other hostile environments; they emerge into an unfriendly world that makes it hard for them to survive decently; they turn more easily to prostitution, dealing, stealing and other illegal activities as a consequence. Whether or not they return home eventually, they generally don't get help for their problems.

Thus the final irony: too many juvenile runaways become emotionally disturbed or unstable adults who raise their own crop of disturbed kids who become runaways. All too often, as one looks at the families of runaways, these transgenerational patterns emerge.

All of this points to the importance of early intervention. Runaway houses are a significant step in that direction. As their funds and administrators allow, many such houses are and should be continuously broadening their base — providing a broad spectrum of crisis intervention services not only for actual runaways but for all local youths, troubled youths, potential runaways. A few — far from enough — have aggressive outreach programs, working with youths on the streets and with the schools in their areas.

Because runaways-to-be often do poorly in school before taking off, schools and runaway houses could form a natural partnership. Teachers are in an excellent position to spot early signs of a problem. Guidance counselors could refer troubled youths to the alternative crisis intervention settings that most such youths prefer over the establishment mental health agencies. (Public school guidance counselors themselves lack the time, and, often, the competence, to do serious counseling.)

Some runaway houses and local schools do carry on joint programs. Berkeley Youth Alternatives, in Berkeley, California, places its counselors and volunteers as interns in five schools; these interns work with chronic truants, heavy drug users and students who create serious disturbances in class. Valley Youth House in Bethlehem, Pennsylvania, gets upward of ten percent of its caseload as referrals from guidance counselors in the area's public schools. Many of these kids don't really need long-term therapy, merely a short cooling-off period because of tensions at home. Dale House in Colorado Springs, Colorado, works closely with the city's high schools. It arranges to have students with learning disabilities tested in the schools, confers regularly with individual classroom teachers and teaches problem students how to relate better to teachers.

However, there are few such joint programs. When the U.S. Office of Education surveyed school superintendents in twenty cities with large runaway populations to find out the kinds of programs available to runaways within the schools, not one superintendent was able to cite even one such program. And only the Superintendent of Schools in Atlanta, Georgia, reported an affiliation between the local schools and an outside agency providing services to runaways.

Joint programs can exist only if runaway houses exist. In 1976 there were no runaway houses in nine states. In many states — Arkansas, Kentucky and Louisiana, for instance — there was only one runaway house in the entire state. Even some meccas for young runaways — a prime example is Los

Angeles — had no runaway shelters at all. Ideally, every community should have its shelter and "drop-in" crisis intervention centers for teenagers.

Joint school–runaway-house programs can work only if the schools are interested and cooperative. By and large, school systems tend to be conservative and to look askance at nontraditional settings.

Finally, whether in conjunction with schools or on their own, runaway-house programs can work only to the extent that they're competently run. But the Runaway Youth Act failed to provide specific guidelines for standards and evaluation. And, as already pointed out, too many shelters are not well administered. Vigorous leadership from the top, from the federal government, has also been lacking. There is a classic dilemma involved: on the one hand, making a program too rigid to allow for different conditions in different localities; on the other, letting it operate so loosely as to defy the imposition of standards. Runaway-program administrators, from HEW on down, have not come to terms with this dilemma. They must.

Alternative Living Situations

Where is it immutably writ that parents and offspring must remain together no matter what? Some parent-child conflicts, even with excellent psychotherapeutic intervention, defy the kind of resolution that has everyone living peaceably under the same roof. Because of temperamental differences some parents and some teenagers will never get along. Yet, viewing their children in some sense as "property," and unable to accept the implicit rejection, many mothers and fathers are highly resistant to the idea of their children living elsewhere, even when those same children forcefully press for a change of that kind. Then a runaway episode occurs and they can't understand why it happened.

"There's such a stigma attached to kids' living elsewhere," Dr. James Gordon of NIMH says. "I try to make parents see it as more of a natural event, their children living elsewhere. Up to a hundred years or so ago kids weren't expected to live at home during adolescence — they stayed with relatives, in boarding schools. What I say to parents is 'Look, you may not be getting along now, and you may continue not to get along if you go on living in the same house. But maybe if you live separately you'll be able to build some kind of relationship.' It's happened with lots of kids I know."

There are parents and children who do work things out positively, of course. In some instances sympathetic relatives who live elsewhere, and who understand the youths involved, act as substitute families. In some instances a sympathetic family friend or the parents of one of the child's friends provide a substitute home. Occasionally two families, each with a troubled and troublesome youth, effect an imaginative exchange: the two kids trade homes on the theory that youths are less likely to be unhappy and hostile with somebody else's parents than with their own. Sometimes this works. Some older teenagers do well living by themselves and going to school or working — and, indeed, a number of runaway houses do set up independent living situations for appropriate teenagers when their parents approve. Some shelters also operate group homes and, with parental approval, also place youths who would be better off elsewhere in licensed communal and foster homes. This is not simply a matter of shifting youths to different living situations but to ones that make sense in terms of their individual problems and needs.

But alternative settings of whatever kind are very scarce. It is much, much easier to find foster parents for pre-adolescents than for teenagers. (Many foster parents reject adolescents out of hand as potential troublemakers.) Relationship problems between adolescents and their foster parents also sometimes erupt, of course, and youths run from foster homes, too. Often this occurs because the foster parents aren't adequately screened, trained or monitored.

Such problems could be ameliorated if more funding was available for alternative living situations for adolescents. Yet how is funding to become more generous if the interest isn't there?

Help for Adult Runaways

Restless, unhappy, disturbed, angry, tormented adults, panicked adults, potential adult runaways, have more options available to them than do their teenager counterparts. Preventive options. Unless they're overwhelmed by circumstances and see running as the only alternative, they can avail themselves of help. Family service agencies. Mental health clinics. Outpatient clinics attached to hospitals. Private therapists and counselors. Even consumer credit counseling services for the heavily indebted (financed and run, it must be said, by some of the same outfits that encouraged the indebtedness in the first place). A variety of establishment agencies that teenagers are apt to reject.

Restless adults who have the money can arrange for styles of life that make them feel less stifled. They can arrange vacations for themselves two or three times a year, instead of taking off on a holiday only once in a big chunk. They can rent rooms or small apartments for themselves — refuges that are completely their own when, for whatever reasons, they feel the need to distance themselves temporarily from their families. Depending on their own talents and the availability of jobs, restless adults, adults who feel confined in the same old setting, might consider a switch in employment, or might consider getting jobs that require travel and would let them indulge their wanderlust without breaking up their families and becoming wanderers or floaters.

Potential runaways who are still only fantasizing about running but who feel overwhelmed by tensions at home might consider arranging a short cooling-off period instead — staying with friends or relatives, renting a furnished room, getting a hotel room. Cooling off in such a setting is much more conducive to ordering one's confused thoughts and doing some clear assessing of the problems at hand than running away, which brings so many new problems to bear.

Much more could be done in terms of setting up shelter facilities for certain types of runaways. Young adults from eighteen to twenty-three or so serve as an example. They're too old for runaway houses. Yet many of them do run from home in the sense that they leave precipitously, in great distress, and aren't prepared to cope with the outside world. The Family Service of Dedham, in Massachusetts, has been considering setting up a group home for young floaters as well as young unmarrieds who are still living at home, not working, not studying, not doing much of anything, not able to separate from Mommy and Daddy. But funding for such projects is difficult to obtain.

Runaway wives are another category of runaways who need more help. A few wives who leave their families now go to women's centers for assistance and are taken in by sympathetic sisters. But the women's centers could establish and administer group homes for runaway wives. In many localities, they're badly needed. There is certainly a need for a more even-handed approach to mission-type shelters, for the current approach is sexist: most existing shelters operate on the philosophy that only men are down-and-outers.

It is not the object of this book to propose specific programs. But I hope I have given ample evidence of the fact that we need to pay more attention, provide more services, for our runaways. For they are "ours" — our children, our husbands, our wives, our parents and, sometimes, ourselves.

Where to Get Help

HOT LINES. At this printing there are two toll-free numbers: "Operation Peace of Mind," 1-800-231-6946, in Texas, 1-800-392-3352; and "National Runaway Switchboard," 1-800-621-4000, in Illinois, 1-800-972-6004.

DIRECTORY OF RUNAWAY HOUSES. Write to National Youth Alternatives Project, 1346 Connecticut Avenue, Washington, D.C. 20036.

FAMILY SERVICE AGENCIES. For the family service agency nearest you, write to Family Service Association of America, 44 East 23d Street, New York City, N.Y. 10010. You can also look under "Social Service Agencies" in the Yellow Pages of your telephone directory.

FAMILIES ANONYMOUS, INC. P.O. Box 344, Torrance, California 90501.

TRAVELERS AID AGENCIES. Look for "Travelers Aid" listings in the White Pages of your local telephone directory, or under "Social Service Agencies" in the Yellow Pages.

Source Note

CHAPTER 2: For the deserted wives in Britain, see "Deserted Wives," in *The Economist* (August 14, 1971). The teenage runaways in Russia are described in "Dropouts on the Run," *Atlas* (March 1966). For both Hammurabi and Rhode Island, see "When Husbands Run Away," *Rotarian* (June 1952). Judge DeLacy can be found in "Family Desertion and Non-Support," *Survey* (February 5, 1910). For the United Hebrew Charities, see C. Zunser, *The National Desertion Bureau, Its Function, New Problems and Relations with Local Agencies* (New York: National Desertion Bureau, 1924); and "Husbands Who Leave Home," *Nation's Business* (February 1951). The Glasgow situation is discussed in "Probation for All Emigrant Husbands," *Survey* (June 21, 1913). For the girls in the Depression, see "Girls on the Road," *Independent Woman* (October 1934).

CHAPTER 3: Runaway statistics are in the National Center for Health Statistics, *Behavior Today* (newsletter, March 26, 1975). See also *Runaway Youth in the Washington Area: A Report* (Washington, D.C.: Metropolitan Washington Council of Governments, October 1974), and *Runaway and Street Children in Massachusetts: A Report* (Boston, Massachusetts Committee on Children and Youth, February 1973). On the legal status of runaways, see W. B. Beaser, *The Legal Status of Runaway Children: A Report* (Washington, D.C.: Educational Systems Corp., April 1975); and *The Child and the Law* (New York: Public Affairs Pamphlets, 1975).

CHAPTER 4: The Forever Family is described in *Time* (March 1, 1976). Runaway-house problems are discussed in "Running Away from Home," *Journal of Social Issues* (vol, 30, no. 1, 1974).

CHAPTER 5: Adolescent abuse is discussed in *Child Abuse and Neglect Reports,* U.S. Department of Health, Education, and Welfare, Publication No. (OHD) 76–30086. The Framingham Court Clinic study is published in "The Runaway Girl: A Reaction to Family Stress," *American Journal of Orthopsychiatry* (vol. 34, p. 762, 1964). For the Shellow Report, see "Suburban Runaways of the 1960's," Society for Research in Child Development (vol. 32, no. 3).

CHAPTER 6: On addictive love, see Stanton Peele, *Love and Addiction* (New York: Taplinger Publishing Co., 1975). For welfare information see *The New York Times,* June 15, 1975.

CHAPTER 9: For counterculture youths today, see *The New York Times,* February 29, 1976. For Dr. Goldberg's study, see "The Runaway Americans," *Mental Hygiene* (January 1972).

A selection of books published by Penguin is listed on the following pages.

For a complete list of books available from Penguin in the United States, write to Dept. DG, Penguin Books, 299 Murray Hill Parkway, East Rutherford, New Jersey 07073.

For a complete list of books available from Penguin in Canada, write to Penguin Books Canada Limited, 2801 John Street, Markham, Ontario L3R 1B4.

THE DIVIDED SELF

R. D. Laing

The Divided Self is a unique study of the human situation. Dr. R. D. Laing's first purpose is to make madness and the process of going mad comprehensible. In this, with case studies of schizophrenic patients, he succeeds brilliantly, but he does more; through a vision of sanity and madness as "degrees of conjunction and disjunction between two persons where the one is sane by common consent," he offers a rich existential analysis of personal alienation. The outsider, estranged from himself and society, cannot experience either himself or others as "real." He invents a false self, and with it, he confronts both the outside world and his own despair. The disintegration of his real self keeps pace with the growing unreality of his false self until, in the extremes of schizophrenic breakdown, the whole personality disintegrates.

SELF AND OTHERS

R. D. Laing

To understand the pressures of conformity we must understand how insidiously they work. To develop genuine, creative relationships we must be aware of a person's capacity to inhibit, control, or liberate another. In this study of the patterns of interaction between people, Dr. Laing attempts to unravel some of the knots in which we unfailingly tie ourselves. He shows that "every relationship implies definition of self by other and other by self" and that if self does not receive confirmation by its contacts with others, or if the attributions that others ascribe to it are contradictory, its position becomes untenable, and it may break down.

THE SECOND TIME AROUND
Remarriage in America

Leslie Aldridge Westoff

One in three marriages ends in divorce, and four out of five divorced people remarry, so the resulting number of remarriages is high indeed —and most of those people have children as well as partners old and new. How do you deal with ex-spouses, new spouses, former parents-in-law, other people's ex-spouses, stepchildren—and how do they deal with you? These are a few of the questions Leslie Aldridge Westoff covers in this readable and informative book.

THE COUPLE

Edited by Marie Corbin

Social scientists from widely different backgrounds report on the couple today—whether married or unmarried, heterosexual or homosexual. The emphasis is on couples in Britain, the United States, Sweden, Italy, and Japan; the authors explore the various approaches and rituals that characterize these societies' attitudes to love, sex, marriage, separation, and divorce.

BITTERSWEET
Surviving and Growing from Loneliness

Terri Schultz

Written within the framework of the author's own intimate experiences, *Bittersweet* is the frankest, most courageous book yet published about loneliness—and how we can cope with it. This honest book tells us why we often feel lonely in childhood, in marriage, during sexual activity, at parties, at work, among friends—at times when we least expect it. Such feelings are not pathological, are nothing to be ashamed of, says Terri Schultz; they are normal, necessary stages of healthy growth. *Bittersweet* shows us how to accept our loneliness—then, as we stop resisting it, how to use it to our advantage.

WOMAN'S BODY, WOMAN'S RIGHT
Birth Control in America

Linda Gordon

Here is a definitive history of the American woman's long struggle for the right to prevent or terminate pregnancy. Tracing the story through Theodore Roosevelt's attack on "race suicide," Margaret Sanger's pioneering crusade, the opposition of religious groups and male supremacists, and the flowering of today's women's movement, Linda Gordon shows that birth control has always been a matter of social and political acceptability rather than of medicine and technology.

WOMAN'S CONSCIOUSNESS, MAN'S WORLD

Sheila Rowbotham

Here is a new voice in the cause of women's liberation. In *Woman's Consciousness, Man's World*, Sheila Rowbotham traces the development of the new feminine consciousness and examines the social changes that lie behind it. She looks at the role of women within the capitalist state and shows how family life is threatened by existing social norms. For her, the cultural and economic liberation of women is inseparable from the creation of a new society totally free of subordination because of sex, race, or class.

ALL GODS CHILDREN
The Cult Experience—Salvation or Slavery?

Carroll Stoner and Jo Anne Parke

Today thousands of young Americans claim to have found salvation in "cults" like the Reverend Sun Myung Moon's Unification Church or Guru Maharaj Ji's Divine Light Mission. Have they found salvation, however, or have they found only ego-destruction and victimization for purposes that have nothing to do with religion? Journalists Carroll Stoner and Jo Anne Parke traveled around the country, attended rallies, services, and discussions, and interviewed hundreds of present and former cult members and their families as well as psychiatrists, clergymen, sociologists, lawyers, and deprogrammers. Their investigations answer questions that concern all who are interested in young people. What are the cults, and who joins them? Who are the cult leaders, and what are their motives? Why do the members accept such unusual social and sexual regulations? What can parents do to dissuade their children from adherence to cults? What does the future hold for the cult children of the 1970s?

ESCAPE ATTEMPTS
The Theory and Practice of Resistance to Everyday Life

Stanley Cohen and Laurie Taylor

This book is about escapes and escape attempts, but the men and women in these pages are not escaping from the cramped cells of a prison; they are fleeing from the demands of everyday life, from the suffocating press of routine and ritual, from the despair of the breakfast table and the office. Their search is for meaning, novelty, progress, and a sense of their identity, their true selves.